The ANC Women's League

T0170814

OHIO SHORT HISTORIES OF AFRICA

This series of Ohio Short Histories of Africa is meant for those who are looking for a brief but lively introduction to a wide range of topics in African history, politics, and biography, written by some of the leading experts in their fields.

The ANC Women's League

Sex, Gender and Politics

Shireen Hassim

OHIO UNIVERSITY PRESS

ATHENS, OHIO

Ohio University Press, Athens, Ohio 45701
www.ohioswallow.com

First published by Jacana Media (Pty) Ltd in 2014
10 Orange Street
Sunnyside
Auckland Park 2092
South Africa
+27 011 628 3200
www.jacana.co.za

First published in North America in 2015 by Ohio University Press
Printed in the United States of America

Ohio University Press books are printed on acid-free paper ⊚ ™

ISBN: 978-0-8214-2156-7
e-ISBN: 978-0-8214-4526-6

Library of Congress Cataloging-in-Publication Data available

Cover design by Joey Hi-Fi

Contents

Preface

This pocket book is based on research conducted over several years, including archival work and interviews. That work is extensively analysed in my book *Autonomy and Engagement: Women's Organizations and Democracy in South Africa*, published by the University of Wisconsin Press. I am very grateful to Gwen Walker at the Press for permission to use this material.

Writing would be an infinitely more lonely and less rewarding task without the support of WUJWG and OWL. Thanks to both collectives for pushing me beyond theoretical comfort zones and for the lessons in writing style.

My father, Aziz Hassim, was delighted with the Jacana Pocket Book initiative and very happy with my participation. He believed in taking ideas beyond the elite circles of academia. I hope I have done justice to his example of speaking to many publics.

1

Introduction

A powerful idea needs a vehicle: it needs the form of words, the organisation of a movement and the energies of a small band of people to move it from the imaginations of a few to the possibilities of many. Gender equality was just such a powerful idea in South Africa in the twentieth century, and for much of that time the African National Congress Women's League was the symbolic vehicle.

Formed in 1918, and calling itself initially the Bantu Women's League, the ANC Women's League grew from a modest grouping of women into the nationalist movement's official arm for the representation of women. The ANCWL is regarded as both front and centre in the century-long transition to a democracy that rates gender equality a core constitutional value. It has always regarded itself, indeed, as *the* women's movement in South Africa, frequently asserting that it is the vanguard organisation and the only legitimate voice of the women of South

Africa. But, as I hope this little book will show, the history of the league is a more complicated affair, as it was neither the only women's organisation in the political field nor was it an easy ally for South African feminism.

The Women's League was always in conversation, often contentiously so, with other women's organisations and with other women in the ANC itself about what gender equality meant both as a set of ideas and as the framework for a plan of collective action. At the time of its formation, women of all races were already articulating political demands, and in many arenas they were beginning to exercise leadership, albeit not on a national scale. For example, African, Coloured and Indian women rebelled against the imposition of regulations that limited their mobility and their right to live in towns, and African women resisted the imposition of restrictions on traditional activities such as beer brewing. White women had begun to question their lack of political rights by the early years of the twentieth century. Indian women living in indenture took up a range of issues relating to conditions of work and their status. And working-class women of all races, newly employed in the factories of an industrialising economy, were becoming active organisers in the trade union movement. Their political demands and campaigns sometimes overlapped, but not always, and the organisational forms and modes of mobilisation often differed.

These multifarious activities suggest that a singular

history of the South African women's movement is not possible. The ANCWL is not *the* taproot of the women's movement, nor should its political dominance be read to indicate the hegemony of its ideas or the class and racial inclusivity of its membership. For much of its history, the league disavowed feminism, and it was never fully able to corral gender activism under its banner. On the contrary, for much of its history, feminists in the ANC could be distinguished from the members of the league, and its most vociferous critics were from within its own party – feminists who understood the political task as involving a radical overhaul of the economic and social relations of gender.

It is fashionable to talk of the present state of the ANC in terms of loss and disillusionment, and to characterise the organisation and its affiliates as having betrayed the earlier democratic values for which the movement so valiantly fought. Foremost in this narrative of loss is the way in which the ANCWL appears in recent years to have abandoned the project of gender equality. Such an approach, however, not only does an injustice to the history of contestation and debate within the movement, but also misrepresents what is at stake in contemporary politics. To be sure, the inclusion of an equality clause in the South African Constitution owes much to the efforts of the ANCWL and feminists within the ANC, and the league may (erroneously) see itself as the guardian of that clause. Yet the past two decades have amply demonstrated the limits of a reliance on vanguardist organisations and the importance of more robust processes of democratic debate. Nowhere is this more apparent than in discussions of gender equality.

A central part of the project for a democratic South Africa was the idea that women would be equal citizens, with all the attendant rights of personhood, dignity and status. In the context of the South African legal system then obtaining, this was a very significant demand. Through most of the country's history, women were considered legal minors, regardless of their race. This applied particularly to married women, whose husbands had extensive marital powers. African customary marriages treated women wholly as minors, even when their marriages ended, and polygamous marriages carried no legal protection for the women involved in them. The idea, central to customary law, that marriage was not a contract between two individuals but part of the unfolding of relationships between different families reinforced the barriers to women claiming any individual rights. So pervasive across race and cultures was the dominance of men in matters of personal and public life that Albie Sachs was moved to comment that 'patriarchy was the only nonracial institution in South Africa'. Of course, women experienced patriarchy through the intersecting systems of racial oppression – in its colonial, segregationist and apartheid forms – and the exploitation of capitalism. The struggle against the oppressions of gender could not be separated from those against class and race oppressions, and the ANCWL positioned itself as the voice of the most oppressed of women. It was a progressive move that should not be underestimated: the league was central to the emergence of gender consciousness in the ANC and in society more broadly.

In the context of the national liberation movement, the emphasis of the Women's League was twofold: to win equality for women within the ANC, and to mobilise women against apartheid. Its track record was uneven. Inside the ANC, it came up against entrenched male entitlement to power and, especially when faced with radical demands from its own constituency, it frequently struggled to formulate a response. Facing outwards to the apartheid state, the league was much more successful in mobilising a mass base for the democratic opposition and in defining the symbolic language of opposition, one which relied on the heroism of women. The league was absolutely central to the embedding of the ANC in the political languages and culture of South Africans, an aspect of its contribution that is frequently underestimated in assessments of the ANC. At a time when the apartheid state was bent on presenting the movement as one of hotheads, saboteurs and terrorists, it was the indisputable strength and heroism of women in the movement that gave the lie to the state's ideology. ANC women stood for justice and a peaceful end to apartheid, and they stood for the collective good of society: that was the clear message sent at every funeral of a fallen cadre when the women sang.

The league could not address those questions by itself, not least because its position as a subordinate member within the ANC's nationalist family limited the framework through which the 'woman question' could be debated. Participation in the ANC enabled women activists to universalise the demand for gender equality within the vision of national liberation. For many (but not all), this became a basis on which to articulate a larger vision of a society in which sex and sexual preference would not matter for the ways in which power was distributed.

At stake was not only the question of whether women could be political actors and the extent to which they would be equal to men within political organisations, but the very definition of what constituted politics. Did inequalities that arose from within the private domain of family and household matter in shaping the political platform of the ANC? Were sex and sexuality appropriate to debates about nation? What was to be done with forms of traditional institutions – public (such as traditional leaders) and private (such as marriages, customary as well as civil) – that relied on and reproduced inequalities of gender? For feminists (though they may not have labelled themselves as such) in the ANC, the project of equality was more than one of mobilising the masses against apartheid. It lay in the eradication of the bases of gender inequality: the lack of recognition of women as

14

full political and sexual agents, the unequal distribution of labour in the home, male control of reproduction and sexuality, and the hyper-exploitation of women in the workplace.

But those forms of gender oppression could not be easily articulated in the Women's League – they found their home in other areas within and around the ANC. In large part, this was because the contours of the league's work were defined within the authorising frame of nationalism, a frame that was inherently limited in its capacity to respond to demands that questioned the social hierarchies that underpinned the political power of men. The increasing embeddedness of the women's movement in the national liberation movement made it difficult to challenge nationalism's reliance on women as the subordinate subject, and to consider forms of sexuality and gender identity that did not fall within the heterosexual norm. Even when women themselves rejected control of their labour and constrictions on their mobility, the league could not match their pragmatic radicalism with an appropriate language, nor channel it in directions that would strengthen more thorough-going changes in the social and economic system.

In dealing with those concerns, the league's performance has been less than stellar. Its status as the official vehicle for women fighting against apartheid concealed many tensions throughout the twentieth century about whether or not feminism was a legitimate frame for women's political activities. The explicit development of feminist ideological frameworks for politics and non-hierarchical forms of activism was circumscribed by the league's concern that assertions of feminism might be read as anti-ANC. As a result, an intellectual and political process that can be traced through two centuries and that had the potential to emerge in a distinctly South African form through the second half of the twentieth century was constantly hemmed in by the need to remain within the fold of nationalism.

At several points in its history, the league initiated or supported coalitions. Two such stand out: the Federation of South African Women in the 1950s, and the Women's National Coalition in the 1990s. In both these cases, the cumulative effect was a substantial shift in the nature of politics and in the ideas that shaped debates in the public sphere. In both these periods, the organisational vehicle of a coalition allowed the league to transcend obstacles within the ANC and weaknesses in its own leadership, and mobilise a larger constituency of women behind the idea of gender equality. A more recent venture, the Progressive Women's Movement, has not yet exerted a major impact on contemporary politics.

The most serious consequences of the antagonism to feminism have become evident in the past two decades. Since 1994 the league has failed to articulate a set of consistent pro-equality arguments, it has not been able to provide clear political leadership for the women's movement and it has dramatically fallen out with feminists even within its own party. It has been most adept at ensuring that there is increasing equity in the distribution of posts in government and its associated institutions. Despite that access to decision-making, and despite the array of bodies at the disposal of the project of equality (such as the Office on the Status of Women and the Commission for Gender Equality and most recently the Ministry for Women, Youth, Children and People with Disabilities), the league has not been able to advance clear policy positions strategically through the ANC government. This failure is not because it 'betrayed' the cause of gender equality but is rather a predictable outcome of its historical tendency to turn its face away from feminism. We should not be too surprised that, in the words of Vuyiswa Tulelo, erstwhile powerhouse in the ANC Youth League, the Women's League is little more than 'a bargaining council for quotas'.

2

Beginnings

In 1912, the newly formed African National Congress had little to say on the question of the role of women in the organisation, and there is scant archival material on which to base specific conclusions about the idea of gender equality. John Tengo Jabavu, one of the founding members of the body, is recognised by the ANC as a champion of women, primarily because he supported the right of women to be educated. That thoroughly modern impulse of improvement runs through all the early ANC literature. Yet the idea that women might use that education to shape their demands for citizenship seems to have eluded the early leaders of the ANC.

It did not, however, elude a newly educated emerging female elite. Among them was Charlotte Manye Maxeke, the first African woman to obtain a bachelor's degree in 1901, from Wilberforce University in Ohio. Charlotte Maxeke's biography exemplifies the kind of women who would lead the ANC Women's League: she was a teacher, a social worker, a woman from a small rural town who seized the opportunities offered by Christian missionaries to craft a new world. In Maxeke, we can see the ways in which, in the early twentieth century, the confines of domesticity could be breached by the opportunities offered by education and (more problematically, given its coercive aspects) paid labour. The world of politics was male, a 'congregation of chiefs and gentlemen', as Cherryl Walker puts it, for whom the exclusion of black men from power was self-evidently wrong but the exclusion of women was unremarkable. Natasha Erlank argues that the ideas of modernity advanced by the urban black middle class depended on the maintenance of gender difference. 'Female autonomy and independence were seen as inimical to proper family life.' Erlank quotes R.V. Selope Thema, a prominent early ANC member, as saying that 'this claim to equality with men by Bantu women is at the root of the destruction of Bantu family life ... No community in which the men are without control over their women can hope to build up a healthy society.'

For women like Maxeke, however, improving the social and economic position of women would be to the benefit of society as a whole. Speaking at Fort Hare University College in 1930, she exhorted her audience: 'If you definitely and earnestly set out to lift women and children up in the social life of the Bantu, you will find the men will benefit, and thus the whole community, both white and black.' Maxeke's speech is a remarkable assertion of the democratising effects of women's rights on society and of the nonracialist impulse that can be found in many aspects of women's political campaigns in the twentieth century.

As Julia Wells has shown, it was pass laws that created the spark for a new form of politics of gender. Passes were a form of legislative control over labour mobility, and an instrument to maintain cheap labour. Although various forms of passes had been used in the nineteenth century, the system was revived in the early twentieth century as a specific form of control of the African presence in the urban areas and mining towns. To be an African without a pass in such an area was to be a criminal. The pass forced Africans into paid labour and then trapped them in relations of employment at the behest of their employers.

African women were not subject to pass laws before the 1890s, and early migrancy was largely a male phenomenon. It was assumed that the primary place of residence of African women was in the rural reserves, subsidising the reproduction of cheap labour. It was indeed a patriarchal bargain between chiefs and white capitalists in which male African labour would be provided and female productive and reproductive abilities confined to the rural sphere. The economic growth precipitated by the discovery of gold and diamonds presented a conundrum to white rule. In the Free State in particular, where African women had moved to urban areas and sought paid labour, the relations between urbanisation, social reproduction and survival were thrown into tension.

The lives of the educated and aspirant African middle-class woman and the working-class woman were cast together in the urban milieu, and it was in the alliance between these two classes of women that the kernel of the twentieth-century women's movement is to be found. As Wells argues, no matter what her class, in the cities the life of an African woman was circumscribed by the restrictions of pass laws. It was a lever used to ensure that women took ill-paid and strenuous jobs as domestic workers, to control choice in the forms of employment, and to expose women to the full force of a racist and sexist police force.

With male leaders of the newly formed South African Native National Congress (which renamed itself the ANC in 1923) seemingly unwilling to take up the issue of passes for women, women took up the cause on their own behalf. In 1912, they petitioned the various provincial governments (of the Cape and the Free State) to repeal existing laws. On their own initiative, they met with a government minister to present a 5000-signature petition against passes. Their arguments against passes referenced equality, but also articulated a demand to end sexual abuse by police. Women joined the branches of the SANNC, and sent women representatives along with the male delegates from the small towns to attend meetings of the organisation in Bloemfontein. By the next year, their appeals to the national and Free State provincial governments had fallen on deaf ears; indeed the women of Bloemfontein found themselves targeted for police action to a much greater extent. In May 1913, a passive resistance campaign was launched in Waaihoek location in Bloemfontein; by June it had escalated into a full-out clash between women and the police, with sticks being flourished by the demonstrators, some of which 'came down with no gentle thwacks across the skulls of the police'.

And so a movement was born.

By the end of the First World War, the involvement of women in the public world of politics had become so commonplace that a national organisation of women seems, in retrospect, obvious. Some accounts date the formation of the Bantu Women's League to 1912, claiming retroactively that the anti-pass campaigns in 1913 were organised by that body, while others cite the formation of the Bantu Women's League as a branch of the ANC in 1918. Charlotte Maxeke was the first president of the first national organisation for black women in South Africa.

Despite women's activism, the ANC did not see women as political agents and perhaps not even as part of their core constituency. Women's status within the ANC was that of auxiliary members, with no voting rights. The women members of the ANC comprised the wives of men who were members of the movement and 'other distinguished African ladies', and their duties were 'to provide suitable shelter and entertainment for delegates to the Congress'. Frene Ginwala has commented that 'men assumed, and women conceded, that defining and achieving the long term goals was men's territory'. Not that this prevented women from making interventions in all manner of public debates. For example, Maxeke was part of the group that founded the Industrial and Commercial Workers' Union (ICU) in 1920, and in 1929 she represented the league at a conference of the liberal Joint Council of Europeans and Bantu. Maxeke successfully argued that women should be full members of the ICU, and delegates at the formation of the trade union resolved that there should be equal pay for equal work. The historian Iris Berger characterises Maxeke as 'a lone voice of female consciousness within a group of men whose primary interests lay elsewhere'.

For all that Maxeke was regarded as the very model of the modern African woman, the ANC leadership stopped short of supporting gender equality outright. In the 1930s Prime Minister J.B.M. Hertzog's proposal to remove African people in the Cape from the common voters' roll, for example, provided an opportunity to debate the nature of the demand for citizenship. The All African Convention, an umbrella body of which the ANC was one among several member organisations formed to fight the so-called Hertzog Bills, called a meeting in December 1935 where the citizenship demand was debated. As

Erlank shows, the discourse focused on the ways in which the denial of the franchise to African people emasculated African men and undermined their ability to care for their families. The extension of the franchise to white women, which parliament had enacted in 1930, reinforced the view that black men were considered uncivilised by the white population. Discussions about black women's rights to vote were minimal, although Dr A.B. Xuma, who would become ANC president in 1940, did cite Maxeke as an example of 'non-European women who are fit to vote'.

During the Second World War, the labour needs of an expanding secondary industry and the decline of the rural reserve economy accelerated women's urbanisation, and, as members of deprived urban communities, women 'formed a significant part of the groundswell of discontent and resistance that rumbled through the townships' in the 1940s, according to Cherryl Walker. Protests against the incursions of township authorities on the activities of African people, demands for affordable housing or transport, and food riots were frequently led by women, and escalated into much larger community mobilisation. Although these political activities were formulated and pursued independently of the Women's League, the militancy among women had an impact on the league. As the women's wing of the national liberation movement, the league increasingly adopted a representative role, and the ferment among women helped it to build up a mass membership for the ANC. In the process, women (and their rights) became central to defining the modernity of the ANC.

By the 1940s women of all races had begun to participate to some extent in the public world of politics. In Natal, Indian women, conventionally understood as publicly quiet and culturally subordinate to men, began to mobilise as part of the passive resistance campaign, originally inspired by Gandhi, to oppose the Asiatic Land Tenure and Indian Representation Act of 1946 (the so-called Ghetto Act). The Ghetto Act prohibited Indians from acquiring fixed property in certain areas, and gave them a limited right to elect white representatives to parliament. Indian women activists such as Dr Kesavaloo Goonam organised women by language – Tamil, Gujarati and Hindi – and drew connections between the struggles of Indians and Africans against white domination while raising the issue of women's rights. Fatima Meer pointed out that 'the Europeans consider Indian women to be at such a low level and to be so ignorant that we are not given the vote'. The limited franchise rights that allowed Indians to be represented by whites, she said, were 'like a wax doll placed in the hands of a woman who were told it was a real life baby. It would not work. It is merely a farce.' Like the ANC, at the time the Natal Indian Congress (NIC) was not convinced that women should have equal rights. When Dr Goonam approached NIC leaders to seek representation for women within the organisation, they told her that 'Indian women were not sufficiently advanced to receive representation'. Attempts were made to form an Indian women's association, but it does not seem to have materialised.

Among white women, as well, urbanisation and independent paid labour had, from early in the twentieth century, produced a new band of female political actors. One such, for example, was Mary Fitzgerald, popularly known as Pickhandle Mary, who formed the Women's Industrial League in 1918, targeting waitresses and laundry workers as members. Among middle-class white women, a suffrage movement emerged in 1911, called the Women's Enfranchisement Association of the Union (WEAU). One of its founders and its first vice-president was the renowned writer Olive Schreiner. As Cherryl Walker points out, Schreiner may have been a socialist but the organisation was determinedly and exclusively white. Their early commitment to votes for all women collapsed under the weight of racism, and they had neither the support of working-class white women nor that of middle-class black women. Radical white women workers later joined the Communist Party and the trade unions. They would become the bedrock of the Federation of South African Women, formed in the 1950s.

Trade unions were the space in which women's militancy was most marked, and in which a growing sense of class solidarity developed in ways that transcended racial differences. Although initially driven by white women, trade unions – as Iris Berger demonstrates –

began militantly taking up shopfloor issues by the end of the 1930s, with radical demands for working women of all races. Among these demands, for example, were equal pay for equal work, prohibition of abuse in the workplace, housing and maternity leave. Black women, too, began to organise workers in sectors such as domestic service.

As a more ambitious leadership emerged within the ANC, the idea that women might be political actors gained some traction. Under the presidency of Dr A.B. Xuma (1940–9), the ANC was put on a course of change from being an elitist organisation to a mass-based movement with functioning branch structures. Xuma's American wife, Madie Hall Xuma, was a powerful force in this process. Madie Xuma was a social worker who fundraised for the ANC in the United States, formed the Zenzele self-help movement and led the league from 1943 to 1948. In this period, the special status accorded to chiefs in the ANC was abolished and women achieved recognition in the ANC. Many felt that Congress was trailing behind the real changes in women's status in the early part of the twentieth century, and that the time had come for women to be recognised as important members. In 1943, thirty-one years after the ANC's formation, women were allowed to become full members of the movement, with rights to vote and participate in all levels of its deliberations. Even then, as a substructure of the ANC, the league remained under the political direction and control of the Congress.

Taking on the struggle against passes, and influenced

by the emergence of radical voices among women of all colours, the Women's League took a much more central role in organising women and in advocating gender equality. In this role, the league wanted much greater autonomy to shape its campaigns and establish its own branch structures but it came straight up against the idea of a centralised movement promoted by the ANC leadership. In 1945 the executive committee of the ANC Women's League passed a resolution asking that it be allowed to 'organise autonomous branches wherever they so desire within the ANC'. This was not allowed, and in 1946 the *ANC Bulletin* pointed out that allowing women to establish the league 'does not mean parallelism but cooperation and mutual assistance in the building up of membership and funds for both sections'.

The place of the league was clear within the nationalist movement. The Congress was a political family and it replicated the hierarchical form of a patriarchal institution, with the exclusively male National Executive Committee acting as the paternal head of the movement, the Women's League playing the lesser, maternal role and the Youth League treated as a space of radical militancy needing the guidance of the parents. Women's political roles were to be defined through the mode of maternalism, acting on behalf of their husbands and children. That early conceptualisation of the nature of women's activism became a chafing point in the years to come. Already by the end of the 1940s, there was impatience with the middle-class style and content of the league under Madie Hall Xuma, and in 1949 the Youth League member Ida Mtwana ('moving spirit among women, orator and heckler') took over as president. Under Mtwana, the league started to root itself among ordinary working-class women in townships. For such women, it was not the self-help groups promoted by Xuma that made sense; rather, they were concerned with the restrictions on the mobility and economic activities of women imposed by the new apartheid system.

3

The idea of a nonracial national women's movement

In the late 1940s and early 1950s the increased activism of women in the ANC and the Communist Party, and the very close working relationships that were developing between women of all races, opened discussions about the possibility of a national women's movement. The obstacle to simply broadening the league's membership base was that the ANC was opposed to this from the start and had decided in 1943 that it would not submerge the ANCWL into a general nonracial women's movement. That would go against the model of organisation that the ANC was developing at the time in which each 'racial' group – Africans, Indians, Coloureds and whites – organised under its own structures but worked together in the so-called Congress Alliance. Like the ANC, the Women's League also drew only African members. Jon Soske shows that in reality there was considerable antagonism to a single nonracial movement based on the historical experience of racism expressed by other groups towards Africans, something not easily overcome even among the progressive leaders of the ANC. The Communist Party was much more strongly committed to nonracialism, and its imprint on the growing women's movement was very strong. Besides, the idea of an autonomous mode of organising was simply not acceptable to the ANC, and the league would have to find some other format for a women's movement. That vehicle would be the Federation of South African Women. The new organisation of women's groups was to be an equal partner in the Congress Alliance.

The idea of a movement in which gender transcended racial and class differences had been brewing for some time among women political activists. The roots of this idea lay in the unions and the Communist Party, in which working-class women had been organised across race, and activists like Ray Alexander and Hilda Bernstein had eschewed the privileges of both their race and class to join in the struggle for socialism. The federation was formed in 1954 at a meeting attended by members of the ANC Women's League, the Communist Party and trade unions. The federation was a nonracial coordinating body to which different groups affiliated. Immediately the question arose about why an organisation of women separate from the ANC was necessary. The central issue was the worry that a women's organisation that was autonomous from the ANC might compete with the league for members and might in fact attract support away from the control of the national liberation movement. In any case, the numbers of women participating in political activities were small and it was not clear that the basis existed for two different organisations. Yet there was a powerful sense that the time was right for a political movement of women. Hilda Bernstein recalled that the federation reflected 'both the idea that women have common interests, and also a strong political attitude'.

At its inaugural meeting the Federation of South African Women adopted a 'Women's Charter', which laid out the political role of women. Although firmly located within the anti-apartheid struggle, the charter also sought to address the specifics of women's oppression: 'The law has lagged behind the development of society; it no longer corresponds to the actual social and economic position of women. The law has become an obstacle to the progress of the women, and therefore a brake on the whole of society. This intolerable condition would not be allowed to continue were it not for the refusal of a large section of our menfolk to concede to us women the rights and privileges which they demand for themselves. We shall teach men they cannot hope to liberate themselves from the evils of discrimination and prejudice as long as they fail to extend to women complete and unqualified equality in law and in practice.' As this excerpt from the charter highlights, the struggle against women's oppression was not simply parallel to the struggle for the rights of black people, but was also a challenge to the deeply entrenched gender hierarchies within black (and other) communities. The charter reflected the tension between mobilising women for national liberation and for women's liberation – a tension that Cherryl Walker's study of the federation shows was resolved by allowing the push for national liberation to dominate. It was a pragmatic decision, though: the federation's membership was primarily drawn from the ANC Women's League, which retained enormous influence within the new body.

The influence of the women from the Communist Party was very clear in the kinds of issues taken up by the federation. The party had pursued very successful campaigns for access to affordable food in the late 1940s, particularly in Cape Town, and brought together women of all races under the motto 'Today we fight for food, tomorrow for the vote and for freedom for all'. The Communist Party was interested in mobilising people around what were called 'bread and butter' issues and focused on drawing the links between working people of all races against racial capitalism. Its leadership reflected this: Hilda Watts (white), Ray Alexander (white), Josie Mpama (African), Rahima Ally (Coloured), Dora Tamana (African). Although most of the African women leaders were also members of the league, their experience of working with white trade unionists and communists made the idea of a nonracial organisation seem both feasible and desirable.

The federation participated in a number of campaigns organised by the Congress Alliance. In 1955 it launched an independent militant campaign against the extension of passes to women that would regulate their urban mobility. The heart of the protest was a massive march of women from around the country to the Union Buildings in Pretoria. On 9 August 1956, a date that has since become symbolic of women's resistance to apartheid, thousands of women assembled at the Union Buildings, where they presented a petition against passes to the National Party government headed by J.G. Strijdom. The march provided some of the richest symbolism associated with women's struggles in South Africa: the photograph of four women of different races standing outside the locked government office door with twenty thousand individually signed petitions; the song 'Malibongwe Amakhosikhazi' (We Thank the Women), the slogan 'Strijdom, you have touched the women, you have struck a rock, you will be crushed', the image of disciplined defiance (twenty thousand women standing silently in the baking sun), and the passion for the cause (women travelling for days from outlying locations to get to Pretoria, in some cases defying their husbands and fathers and even, by some accounts, defying the ANC).

The women's campaigns against the pass laws spread. Several other 'defiance campaigns' against pass laws led to the arrest of many thousands of women during 1957. The Congress Alliance's response to the scale and nature of the protest was not entirely supportive: the federation's position, enthusiastically supported by the defiance campaigners, was 'no bail, no fines', but the ANC leadership argued that instead of seeking confrontation with the authorities, the federation should concentrate on educational campaigns. Helen Joseph commented that 'we were disappointed and a little angry at first, but we were also disciplined and we were a part of the whole liberation struggle. There was no room for any rebellious spirit on our part and there was none. Bail and fines were paid and the women returned to their homes.' Hilda Bernstein, a Communist Party member and leader of the federation, remarked that 'women were not bystanders, nor reluctant participants dragged along by the militancy of the men, but were an integral part of the whole development of the campaigns. Without their activities, the campaigns could not have taken place.'

The tensions between the ANC's male leadership and the women leaders spilled over into the relations between the league and the federation, exacerbated by the two anti-pass marches. Julia Wells comments that differences over how the marches should be conducted and just how radical the women's demands should be, played a role in undermining the autonomy of the federation: 'Amid continuing charges that the Federation drew support away from the ANCWL, Federation leaders bent over backwards to prove their allegiance to the male-dominated ANC leadership … When Federation members proposed a huge march to deliver their half-million signatures [against passes], they agreed to allow the (male) leaders of the ANC to set the date. No date was ever set and the demonstration never took place, much to the disappointment of many women.'

The movement of women into towns and cities changed the urban landscape and at the same time expanded the constituencies for political mobilisation. Control over urban African lives was challenged by women on a daily basis; their illegal beer brewing, or protest against the extension of passes, for example, exposed the limits of the state and policing. Although too few studies exist of the impact of ordinary women on the agendas of political movements in the early twentieth century, Phil Bonner comments that 'if you look at the histories of the localities, the fragments, women clearly emerge as the driving forces of radical community politics' in the period between the 1930s and the 1950s. Bonner suggests that national and provincial politics were a male domain, while women occupied the local realm, which tended to be regarded as outside politics proper. Noor Nieftagodien makes a similar argument about what he calls the 'spatial division of gender activism', noting that women were more dominant in localised spaces such as backyards while men played a more central role in national politics. These two historians alert us to the ways in which histories that focus only on the ideas and strategic discussions of the nationalist leadership end up missing the complex texture of politics in the first half of the twentieth century. But pushing the analogy of a spatial gender division in the organisation may itself elide the extent to which women did indeed engage in the broader politics of the Union. More accurately, it does not address the possibility that the involvement of women in struggles against racism and class exploitation was marginalised – at times even closed down – by men who could not conceive of women as political actors. It was men who thought that women's domain was that of the local and of the family, while women activists were busy making the crucial links between race, class and gender exploitation.

By 1963, whether as a result of gradual compliance with the male leadership's views on women's roles or the increasing repression following the Sharpeville massacre in 1960, the federation was to all intents and purposes no longer functional in South African politics. While its leading members were banned or placed under house arrest, unlike other political organisations the federation itself was not the subject of a banning order. But those federation leaders who were still alive and living in the country in the early 1980s would have a role to play in the later resurgence of women's political activism and would influence debates far more powerfully than the exiled league.

4

Exile

Ater 1960 the Women's League, driven together with the ANC into exile and officially suspended, had to design new modes of operation and take on an entirely new set of responsibilities.

It is not entirely clear from the archival record why the league decided to suspend its name and the whole of its programme in exile. The constitution of the ANC itself was suspended in exile, which may be the reason. The league reconstituted itself in a partial form in Morogoro, Tanzania, under the leadership of Ruth Mompati, who was part of the ANC's External Mission. From 1969, following the recommendations of the Morogoro Conference, women in the ANC were organised within the Women's Section, headed politically by the Women's Secretariat. In 1971, the Secretariat was led by Florence Mophosho with Magdalene Resha, Edna Mgabaza, Kate Molale and Theresa Maimane as members. Mophosho was transferred from her position as a member of the Secretariat of the Women's International Democratic Federation, an international socialist body of which the ANC had been a member since the late 1940s. From 1981 Gertrude Shope was president of the Women's Section. In 1983 the Women's Secretariat established a substructure called the National Women's Executive Committee, which conducted the day-to-day business of the Women's Section.

The key tasks of the Women's Section were to mobilise women into active membership within the ANC and to campaign for political and material support internationally. Although it was designed to fill the gap left by the suspended Women's League, the Women's Section was organised along different lines. The relative autonomy that the ANC Women's League had begun to delineate in formal terms, if not always in practice, was eroded. The ANC had a massive task in maintaining itself as an exiled political movement, and it was much easier to work under a more centralised leadership.

Even so, the status and powers of the Women's Section were to become a thorny issue in its relationship with the ANC's National Executive Committee (NEC). In addition to the main office in Lusaka, the Women's Section had several regional units, each with at least five members. All women in the ANC in exile were automatically members of the Women's Section. From its inception, its primary role was to act as the movement's social worker, providing social services and a supportive environment for women rather than to represent women politically. Cast in this role, it is not surprising that for almost all of the 1960s and 1970s the Women's Section functioned as a network of solidarity rather than as a mobilising agency. That imprint within the league, going right back to Charlotte Maxeke and continuing into the present in the figure of Winnie Madikizela-Mandela, a trained social worker, defines virtually all the key contests in the league. A social worker impetus is invaluable and worthy, but it is also a potentially conservative framing of what the contributions of women could be within political movements. At times, the caring maternalist role might be the basis for radical politics, as in the 1980s when women were at the forefront of challenging the presence of South African Defence Force troops in the townships. At other times, it drew the league into defining all women's interests as coterminous with those of the family (whether social family or political family).

In exile, although young militants later criticised the social work role of the Women's Section, the care services that it undertook – such as establishing child-care facilities and processing donations of food and clothing – were important to ANC members in the context of exile. For many younger members, the provision of these services allowed feminists in the movement to pursue activist lives even when they had children.

The care of people with personal and physical

difficulties was primarily the responsibility of the Women's Secretariat, and the necessity of these practical activities reinforced its conventional role as a women's auxiliary of the national liberation movement. In this capacity its role was both validated and valuable for the movement. However, this work pushed some women activists to question the extent to which the movement was in practice committed to women's equality and whether in fact women stood to gain equality automatically from national liberation.

Conditions in exile were harsh, particularly for those deployed in African countries. Exiled members of the ANC lived for the most part on meagre funds raised by the movement abroad. In Africa most members did not work for a salary, although everyone regardless of rank received a small stipend, and they relied on the movement for food and shelter. People were moved around according to the needs of the movement. This produced uncertainty and anxiety and reinforced the power over the rank and file of a small elite that controlled resources. For some exiles the psychological burdens were almost unbearable, and the Women's Section offered solidarity and a sense of security very similar to the way in which prayer groups and savings clubs offered newly urbanised women support within South Africa during the early twentieth century. The Women's Section East Africa Region, for example, reported in 1981 that 'many [women] are idle and very anxious about being involved in meaningful activity, either work or school. Some are ill and feel insecure … Others are just going through a difficult stage of readjustment to exile, an abnormal situation that we only fully appreciate when we are already out here … General meetings bring us together to share our views … They also give us a feeling of belonging with one another, which is very essential, especially in exile.'

The Women's Section was responsible for the well-being and education of children of ANC members in exile. It set up and ran various nursery schools, including the Dora Tamana Crèche in Lusaka, Zambia, and the Charlotte Maxeke Mother and Child Centre in Mazimbu, Tanzania. The running of these nurseries was taken very seriously, and numerous training workshops were held on nutrition and child care, for example, for the nursery workers. Although the ANC had a policy of keeping families together whenever possible, many children were separated from their parents, and members of the ANC Women's Section acted as surrogate mothers – in an effort to make the nurseries 'a home and not an institution'.

Mavis Nhlapo (aka Dr Thandi Ndlovu), administrative secretary for the Women's Section in the early 1980s and a protégé of Jack Simons, said that 'the maternal instinct of protection certainly drove the Women's Section'. An MK cadre noted that 'I didn't have to choose between motherhood and politics because the Women's Section made it possible for me to do both. I knew I could leave my child in good hands.' This was a minority view, though:

most women in the movement were very unhappy about being separated from their children.

Despite the emphasis on women's maternal role, motherhood in practice limited women's mobility within the movement. Women members of MK were forbidden to become pregnant. Women deployed to the Angolan camps had IUDs inserted as a matter of policy. 'Some women became infertile as a result. We were told we had to do it because if we fell pregnant we wouldn't be allowed to be there,' Muff Andersson recalled. ANC policy was to send new mothers to Morogoro with their children. Young mothers and babies were sent to the Charlotte Maxeke Mother and Child Centre in Mazimbu, which, while it provided a caring environment, was also 'regarded by the authorities as a way of isolating those who had behaved in an unacceptable way'.

For young women 'there was a slight horror about having children and being sent to Tanzania', where they would spend long months without any activity, according to a study by Sean Morrow, Brown Maaba and Loyiso Pulumane. Women in MK argued that new mothers should 'be flung back into the actively fighting ranks so that childbirth does not become the devastating route to demobilisation'. At the urging of the Women's Section, the Secretary-General's Office agreed in 1981 that day-care centres ought to be established in all ANC bases. To be sure, the ANC was limited by financial constraints in meeting this objective; nevertheless, the Women's

Secretariat pointed out that the consequences were gendered. Women were left with the responsibility to look after children, while male cadres either got on with their revolutionary work free of obligations or became involved with new partners and had other children.

Financial considerations aside, the National Executive Committee of the ANC did not really appear to grasp the political significance of a good child-care system. When the issue was raised by the National Women's Executive Committee in 1984, the ANC's treasurer-general again 'levelled strong criticism over the creation of crèches all over'. The issue continued to trouble women members of the ANC. 'We seem to travel in a dead end street with marriage and babies being at the end of the street. There is not and can never be a contradiction between marriage and having babies on one hand and fighting on the other. There have been revolutions before, women have married and women have borne children during these, but women have fought. We are not and cannot be exceptions,' the Women's Section reported in 1987. These comments represent the kernels of a potentially radical new approach to the social status of women, though ideas of a more egalitarian society did not flourish.

Social welfare problems intensified rapidly after the 1976 uprising, with the sudden influx of young people into ANC camps in Africa. Most were aged fifteen to twenty, and they brought with them the common problems of teenagers everywhere. Inevitably, the Women's Section was left to take care of this group, to act as surrogate mothers. Many of these youngsters had gone into exile with youthful idealism, believing that 'they would be back [home] with Kalashnikovs within six months'. Instead, they found themselves in conditions that were often harsh and with long periods of inactivity while they waited to be transferred to educational institutions in the Eastern bloc, United States or Britain or to military camps. The number of teenage pregnancies increased, and the Women's Section was frequently drawn into resolving personal and relationship problems. 'Torn from their parents, our students, particularly the very young ones, need to be associated with our women as mothers, to guide them particularly in upholding the discipline of the movement. This would go a long way in giving them a sense of belonging and boosting their morale,' the ANC Women's Secretariat reported in 1981.

The Women's Section was asked to organise recreational and cultural activities for young girls, to keep them occupied. Through skills-training workshops the young women learned crafts such as weaving and producing T-shirts and other items for the movement. The Women's Section also counselled students and monitored their progress; such counselling sometimes included assuming the role of moral regulation. Students studying abroad posed their own set of problems. They sometimes defected from the movement, and some women who married foreigners did not report to ANC headquarters for duty after completing their studies. Tensions between male and female students abroad were numerous, caused by the ubiquitous 'relationship' problems. Women students complained that men 'were only interested in getting them drunk and getting them into bed', and the Women's Section was called in to mediate, sometimes as far afield as the Soviet Union.

Young men in the ANC repeatedly attacked women students who went out with foreigners, despite an ANC ban on marriage between ANC women and foreigners. At a meeting of the Women's Secretariat and the Youth Secretariat, the two groups agreed that 'we try very hard to discourage our women getting married to foreigners and a positive attitude of male comrades towards female will help alleviate the problem in the socialist countries. Women must be made to understand their allegiance to the country and our people.' Muff Andersson pointed out that sexist attitudes regarding marriage stemmed from 'the expectation that a woman would follow her husband into his home, so South Africa would lose. If a man marries a foreigner, it will strengthen the South African struggle, but if women married a foreigner it would strengthen the man's struggle.' The control of women also extended to their relationships with South African men who were not members of the ANC. For example, young women who went out with members of the Pan Africanist Congress (PAC) were seen as breaching discipline. In some cases the ANC administered corporal punishment, although the Women's Section advised against it: 'Some of the girls have been [beaten] on their back-sides and some bear scars. But the punishment has not been effective because some of them have gone back to the PAC men.' Later, when the young women were questioned, they said they did not know that the differences between the ANC and the PAC were of a serious nature. The Women's Section preferred that young women be warned and then expelled, and protested strongly (but unsuccessfully) against corporal punishment as a mode of discipline.

As a result of the practical work that the Women's Section took on in relation to women and children in exile, it often proposed that the exiled movement adopt more progressive social policies and strategies. In some respects these ideas predated positions that emerged from women's organisations during the 1990s. For example, health facilities in the camps were inadequately staffed and stocked, and the Women's Section, bearing the brunt of the consequences of this for women and children, felt compelled to assume responsibility for making improvements. But members of the National Executive Committee sometimes questioned the authority of the Women's Section to take on tasks that it saw as within the scope of work of some other body in the ANC, wishing to confine the Women's Section to a narrow understanding of its role. For example, when the Women's Section wanted to expand the work it was doing in the area of health care, the NEC chided: 'Health is a charge of the movement. It is not a women's matter.'

Because of the high pregnancy rate among teenage comrades, the Women's Section took responsibility for sex education and family planning. The Women's Section also recommended that sex education be part of the curriculum at the Solomon Mahlangu Freedom College (Somafco) in Tanzania, although the NEC refused. The Women's Section suggested, somewhat desperately, that 'perhaps the word sex education could be changed'. As Morrow, Maaba and Pulumane have noted, 'the school did not show a sure touch in its approach to sexuality and pregnancy among students'. Another example was the increasing conviction in the Women's Section that abortion should be legalised – again a consequence of the incidence of botched abortions on teenage girls in Lusaka, where abortions were illegal. On this issue, the ANC would act firmly soon after taking power in South Africa, by ratifying the Choice on Termination of Pregnancy Act in 1996.

A significant and widespread problem was violence against women. Women's Section documents carry numerous reports of abuse, with women appealing to the Women's Section for assistance and for discipline to be meted out to abusive men in the movement. This abuse sometimes extended to children. Even worse, in one document the Women's Section notes that 'we hear of a number of children who have had to be stitched heavily having been "punished" by officials of the movement'.

The Women's Section made several unsuccessful attempts to deal with the problem, arguing as late as 1987 that 'a long standing practice, that of women abuse and child battering, has now become common in the ANC. The movement should, with proper directives from this conference, come up with a policy on this negative practice. While waiting for the implementation of the code of conduct, we could use and implement measures taken, otherwise our aim of building and producing responsible cadres of this movement will soon be destroyed and defeated.'

The Women's Section at Mazimbu in Tanzania adopted a policy that 'offending men should be locked up for two weeks, whether or not this was requested by their partners'. Most disturbingly, it was not only men who were violent. In one instance, a matron at Mazimbu was accused of beating a child who had been left in her care while the mother was away on a scholarship. 'The beating was so severe that subsequently the child could neither sit down nor walk properly.' In 1988 a working committee was set up to compile a report because the issue of violence 'has now been considered by the high structures of our movement'. It was also hoped that the newly established Emancipation Desk in the Women's Section, headed by Zanele Mbeki (wife of Thabo Mbeki), would monitor developments, but the problem of violence against women remained an issue for the entire period of exile and, as I will discuss later, continues to be a concern among Women's League members.

The Women's Secretariat also had to deal with the constant movement of its members. All were assumed to be in transit and, at the behest of the movement, might leave to pursue studies, be deployed into MK or accompany a transferred spouse. The result was that for a long time the Women's Secretariat was a very unstable structure. It was hard to build up a core team and to develop its own relationships and contacts with underground activists in the internal women's movement. It received very sporadic information about women's activities inside South Africa and usually relied on intelligence from London, through which a steady stream of internal activists passed. As a result the Women's Section was not always able to follow the 'complex situation' in women's politics inside the country. Under these conditions it was hard for the Women's Secretariat to consolidate – or even conceptualise – a more overtly political role.

The magazine *Voice of Women* (*VOW*), the key propaganda organ of the Women's Section, was intended to provide one of the crucial linkages between internal women's organisations and the exiled movement. It was established in 1971 to mobilise South African women inside and outside the country into ANC structures; to lobby the international community to support the ANC's cause; and to 'take up issues which affect women'. The publication was never very successful. It was produced under extremely difficult conditions in Lusaka:

outdated and barely functioning machinery, poorly trained journalists, and few financial and informational resources. The journal received a boost with the deployment of the astute Mavivi Myakayaka-Manzini in 1981 as its editor and head of the subcommittee on information and publicity; she was complemented by a team that included the trained journalist Marion Sparg. This team was analytically skilled and articulate, but even then problems persisted. Staff would acquire skills, only to be redeployed by the NEC to some other position, with no provision for replacements or consideration of the impact on the activities of the Women's Section. In any case, the code of discipline that operated in the ANC in exile made attempts to shift the parameters of responsibility and accountability over decision-making difficult, if not anathema. One key implication of the lack of skills and continuity was the weakness of the *Voice of Women* and the Women's Section in building effective communication with the internal women's movement. The 1981 conference of the Women's Section, for example, decided that the journal should discuss issues from inside South Africa more fully and take on the task of political education for internal activists.

This was consistent with the general ANC emphasis after 1979 on developing an internal political base rather than relying solely on armed struggle to overthrow the apartheid state. However, the magazine (and the Women's Section itself) did not have up-to-date information on internal developments, and the periodical was not widely circulated inside South Africa. '*VOW* was said not to be giving direction to the problem of organisation of women inside the country which is needed presently. Here it was pointed out ... that due to the lack of information of what is the level of organisation of women at home, the problems existing, and the objective conditions existing it has become very difficult to give such direction. Some time an attempt was made of calling for women to form a national body, and as we were doing it the women at home were calling for the consolidation of regional [*sic*] and formation of regional women's organisation so we were not at par with the women at home.'

The Women's Secretariat noted criticism that *VOW* had 'a weak political content, which makes *VOW* not to match the revolutionary situation in the women's front inside the country. The machineries concerned with the distribution inside the country have complained that *VOW* does not always guide the women in their everyday struggles; but only responds spontaneously on issues taken up. Even then, it does not address itself to the tactics used by women at a particular time, and does not help them to assume higher forms of struggle.'

A key impediment to the ability of the Women's Section to develop a good intelligence network about developments within the country was the limited power of the structure within the ANC. Communications between internal cadres and the movement were governed by the

Revolutionary Council, a body that, until its dissolution in 1983, had no more than one woman member at any given time. The Women's Section was not allowed to have direct links with women inside the country, as the ANC regarded the decentralising of communication networks as a weakening of military discipline. In any case, the mobilisation of women was not seen as a high priority for the Revolutionary Council or its successor, the Politico-Military Council. Consequently, very few such linkages developed, and even these were invariably infiltrated, according to one source. Some women (most notably the trade union organiser Ray Simons) ignored the formal structures and maintained their own contacts but they were often criticised by the male leadership for doing so.

It was only at the first conference of women in exile, in Luanda in 1981, that a clearly defined political position on women began to emerge within the Women's Section. This conference provided an important platform for women in the ANC to debate and assess their strength inside the liberation movement. By this stage there had been a significant influx of young women into the exiled movement following the 1976 Soweto uprising. The Women's Section wanted to take responsibility for preparing fact papers for distribution among women in exile but was limited by resources and by weak networks with women within South Africa. The Women's Section was not encouraged to develop its own intelligence mechanisms, indeed it may have been dissuaded from doing so, and thus relied on very patchy reporting on what the internal women's organisations were doing. This was a somewhat problematic position to be in, given the massive resurgence of women's organisations in Natal and the Western Cape in the late 1970s and early 1980s, and in the Transvaal by 1983. For the internal bodies the absence of support from those in exile was not quite so problematic, as they relied on the advice and support of older women who had been active in the 1950s and stayed inside the country, such as Helen Joseph, Albertina Sisulu, Frances Baard and Dora Tamana. But the model that they drew on was that of the Federation of South African Women, not the league. That is, they were debating the possibilities of creating women's organisations that would develop their own structure, programmes and modes of organising, independent of the control of male-dominated political bodies. In effect, this would shape their relationship to the league and become a source of political tension in the early 1990s, when the league returned from exile.

5

The impact of armed struggle

The movement of significant numbers of young people into the exiled movement after the Soweto uprising in 1976 changed the composition of the ANC and infused new energies into the ageing cohort of exile leadership. Not surprisingly, this situation opened many new areas for internal conflict within the ANC, with gender struggles becoming much more open.

Since its exile the ANC had placed extraordinary emphasis on the role of armed struggle as the primary strategy for challenging the apartheid state. Umkhonto we Sizwe (MK) thus came to constitute the powerhouse of the exiled movement. After 1976 MK, which had been overwhelmingly male in composition, saw a dramatic increase in the number of women combatants, who by 1991 constituted approximately 20 per cent of the army. The women who joined the movement in this period brought new energy and militancy from the townships into the ANC, and particularly into MK. The simple fact of their joining the armed wing acted as a destabilising factor in the most masculine of the ANC substructures, and shaped the ways in which they responded to other more conservative forces within the ANC. Many women had been local leaders of the student movement and 'couldn't be pushed around, they stood their ground'. In their edited collection of Jack Simons's writing, Marion Sparg, Jenny Schreiner and Gwen Ansell suggest that the women were overall more educated than the men, and that this influenced debates in the camps. Thandi Modise, part of the '76 generation and subsequently a commander in Umkhonto we Sizwe in Angola, noted that 'the ANC was really caught off guard, didn't know what to do with us – too many young people coming in, some of them too energetic'. The archetypal MK woman – described by the Women's Section as 'an independent personality who can be seen by her detachment from ego; she has good qualities as a person without self-pity and arrogance' – became an icon of the national liberation struggle.

It is difficult to be precise about the political influence of women in MK as this is an under-researched area. Apart from Jacklyn Cock's groundbreaking account in 1991, Goldblatt and Meintjes's study for the Truth and Reconciliation Commission, and more recent work by Raymond Suttner, sources are thin. In particular, there is little analysis of the political influence on the ANC of the role of women in MK. Cock has argued that 'there is no doubt that women have played an important and courageous part in MK activities. Undoubtedly the nature of the struggle and the breakdown of normal male–female roles encouraged many women to discover new capacities within themselves ... At the same time, the image of the female fighter – the MK guerrilla – has become a popular mass image of the strong, liberated woman.' Indeed, it has been argued that the militarisation of the struggle undermined women's organisation. Albie Sachs, for example, sees the turn to armed struggle as a setback for women. 'The more the struggle focused on armed combat the more it took on a male character and women played an auxiliary role as carriers.' Thenjiwe Mtintso, on the other hand, sees the developments within MK as the beginning of a new process of opening opportunities for women within the ANC, as the movement began to recognise women's contribution. In part this was because of the status MK itself enjoyed within the ANC. 'MK had a rank of its own. [Women were seen] to have a tougher commitment ... They made tough choices and made comradeship stronger,' Mtintso said. 'Women members of MK had to be taken seriously. They had to explode the myth of women as inferior on a day to day basis. They did not articulate feminism but had to prove themselves in the field and gain respect. Women as a collective gained respect out of the performances of individual women. Men had to give respect even if it was grudging.'

Ironically and unwittingly – and despite the resistance

of the military leadership – MK provided an important arena within the movement in which to raise issues of gender equality. Interviewed in the *Voice of Women*, one cadre called MK a 'school of equality'. Although the language of equality was not common parlance, given the rigid hierarchy and emphasis on military discipline that characterised the armed wing, women combatants drew on other aspects of ANC rhetoric to make their claims. As Thandi Modise has argued, 'We said we wanted to be treated like everybody else … They said "And therefore you will dig like every man does and therefore you will do, whatever." And we said "Fine!" So we dug the trenches and the men would sit there and smoke and we dug! It was difficult … our hands! … Your body would ache because in the mornings the road work … they made it extra difficult – going up and down the mountains. We needed to prove we'd keep up … Try to be one of the boys because that is one of the protections you have.'

Women and men received the same political and military training, although women's training was often not as physically rigorous and their roles were not the same. Even though women were often better shots than men, they were not allowed to participate in sniper training, and women were excluded from traditional combat roles. Jack and Ray Simons ran classes for women in the camps, aimed at equipping them not only with theoretical skills but also with the confidence to speak out. The rigorous training was strategic. Jackie Molefe put it bluntly: 'What we try and get across is that when the SADF [South African Defence Force] comes, the cadres will not be able to choose. You must be able to defend yourself.'

While men spent long periods in the camps, women tended to leave very shortly after their training. Instead of combat, women were trained to do courier work. Many women cadres saw this as undermining the commitment to equality, and women in MK demanded that 'there should be no Umkhonto wabafazi [army of women] or wamadoda [of men]'. There was no doubt that life in the camps was physically and psychologically gruelling. As Tom Lodge has noted, 'Placing large numbers of men in holding camps for long periods of inactivity is an almost certain recipe for low morale and indiscipline.' While women demanded equality and respect from their male comrades, they also benefited in some ways from being treated as special cases. On the one hand, the treatment of women as appendages and possessions of men sometimes exposed them to abuse, but, on the other hand, special protection mitigated some of the worst effects of camp life and its anomie. Janet Love, a white activist who joined MK after 1976, commented on the contradictory effects of patriarchal attitudes: 'I was far more fortunate than a lot of other people, and I think that was [because] of a much more conscious effort within MK to generally pay more attention to the sorts of decisions that would need to be taken around women ... There was much more of a conscious effort to make sure that women would be utilised to a greater degree than men. I mean, there were men that stayed in the camps for more than ten years, and I want to tell you that is hideous.'

Tensions within MK over the perceived failure to return trained cadres to South Africa during the early 1980s were enormous. Women cadres were particularly concerned at the low numbers of women sent back to act as underground activists. They argued that 'it has been proven that the chances of survival in the underground for women are greater than for men. People at home have actually demanded/recommended that the ANC should send and train more women.' Molefe's comments to Cock suggest that the acceptance of equality was almost as difficult for the women as for the men: 'Some of the women can't cope with the exercises. It takes some time to convince women; they have hangovers [*sic*] about how a woman should be treated because of their upbringing. In the beginning they expect help or say they can't exercise too much because they will come to have legs like men ... In the beginning the boys expected to have their clothes washed, and the girls would do it.'

Women's presence in MK was by no means easily accepted. Although the high level of commitment of women within MK, and the fact that some women performed better than men in the field and in shooting practice, forced men to recognise women's capacities, women were constantly questioned about 'what [they] were doing in a man's world,' Mavis Nhlapo said.

There was ambiguity about women's formally equal status, on the one hand, and the ways in which traditional gender relationships could offer women both emotional comfort and preferential access to scarce resources, on the other. Janet Love commented that 'things were tough there [in the camps]. You are filled with uncertainty … You know sometimes women were flattered by attention [from male leaders]. Material things then became on offer, you know, sort of the extra trip to town or the extra possibility of going to select items of clothing from jumbles that was sent us by charitable institutions from Europe … And that is also quite undermining. Somehow one asks, "Why am I doing this? Who am I?" Not so much "Why am I MK? Why am I politically involved?" but "Why am I associated with particular people?" You kind of think you got it taped, you think you are doing it for the right reasons, and then you kind of get ambiguous about it.'

In a 1987 report, women in MK complained that 'comrades are in a hurry to "privatize" women because of the shortage of women in MK.' Mtintso commented that 'camps could dull your sharp gender mind, but you also dulled it deliberately. You didn't want to look at roles as exploitative, you deliberately didn't want to see it … Life is tough … you wanted to make your life as comfortable as possible … I could benefit from having a relationship with commanding personnel. If I don't, life is going to be hell. All of us experience hell, men and women, but men bring things from town, goodies.' Sometimes the unequal power relations between men and women slipped into abuse. Mavis Nhlapo noted that women felt they were treated as 'second-class citizens. I was appointed a commissar and so I heard all the problems. I fought hard for the rights of the women. Even some of the senior people took advantage of the girls. I felt they should be setting an example.' Thandi Modise recalled an incident in Tanzania, where there was a fight about the sexual availability of women cadres. 'There was this idea that we [women] needed to be superfit. Against the enemy, the South African state, then, and against men who just wanted to take advantage of us ... But there had been a fight one night over girls ... because there had been a feeling among some men that because there are these five, six women there, why should they [the men] be sex starved? and there were others who said, "No, they are not there to be sex slaves – if they want to have affairs, they will have affairs; if they don't want to, then you are there to protect them."' This was true in other parts of the movement as well. Albie Sachs said that 'the line was "it's simple, we agree with equality". But young women wanting scholarships sometimes had to sleep with people or could be given tasks on the assumption that women were available as sexual partners.'

Clearly, it was not easy to connect the expansion of women's roles and women's status. The 'sharp gender mind' nevertheless shifted the conception of women's status within the ANC. However it was defined, if the concept of equality could be accepted within MK – supposedly, the arena in which the most committed members were located – then it could be extended to other parts of the ANC. Thenjiwe Mtintso pointed out that the significance of women's involvement in MK was that 'women were saying we are full citizens in the ANC'. Not surprisingly, given MK's extremely hierarchical and authoritarian structures, it was also within MK that the limits of rhetorical commitment to equality were most directly experienced. MK was slowest to respond to the demands for greater representation of women in its leadership and least receptive to the need to mobilise women around issues of women's emancipation. While women were making strides throughout the 1980s in other structures of the movement, Nhlapo said, 'the MK side was still a big problem. Post-1981 the leadership of MK did not want the Women's Section involved in the activities of women in MK. This created a lot of bitterness. We felt the women in MK were getting a raw deal – women who were deserving of positions were not getting them. We had several discussions with the NEC, with the Revolutionary Council, with Military Headquarters, we knocked on every door but were told MK is a completely different domain.'

This slowness to respond to concerns about gender equality must be linked to the overall undervaluing in MK of the political aspects of the struggle against apartheid. Although a major strategic review within the ANC in 1978–9 shifted the emphasis from military to political means of struggle, armed struggle remained the bedrock of the ANC's vision of revolution. Issues such as greater independence for the Women's Section in defining relationships with internal women's organisations, and concerns with democratic culture and values that were being slowly articulated by women in the movement, got little attention in MK. Women's frustration with the lack of progress in convincing MK of the need for greater internal democracy translated into dissatisfaction with the structures of women's representation inside the ANC. The difficulties with MK exposed the limited powers of the Women's Section inside the ANC and became the source of tensions between the Women's Section and women soldiers, tensions that pushed debates about organisational autonomy and the role of political mobilisation to new heights by 1987.

The claim of women in MK for 'full citizenship' had implications for the position of women within the movement. In President Oliver Tambo, women had a sympathetic, if paternalistic, leader. Tambo was not a feminist, but he was 'quite liberated, especially for his age. His international experiences broadened his worldview,' Mtintso said. 'He was one of those inherently progressive characters, a revolutionary democrat who lived his beliefs in practice ... He was able to look at women with respect.

They had sacrificed more than men, by leaving home they [women] showed advanced political thinking. He wanted to give everyone the opportunity and ability to play a role.' Albie Sachs made a similar argument about Tambo's role: 'OR's leadership wasn't so much to promote the cause of women as women. He saw himself as a leader of a broad organisation and saw that there was a section of the organisation that was held back. His vision was as a democrat rather than as a nonsexist.'

During Tambo's presidency women gained significant opportunities within the ANC. For example, Tambo appointed several women as representatives of the movement abroad, including Lindiwe Mabuza, Barbara Masekela and Ruth Mompati. These postings gave women an opportunity to demonstrate their skills and also exposed women in the ANC to the rising tide of feminism internationally. For the women based in African countries, the mid- to late 1980s was a period in which 'the question of gender struggle as distinct began emerging. We see reversals in Mozambique, Zimbabwe, and Namibia. For women comrades "normality" meant going back to the kitchens,' Mtintso remarked. 'We began to be quite worried about what liberation was going to offer.'

6

Feminism in the ANC

Thenjiwe Mtintso's concern about the future was also rooted in an awareness of the difficulties of women having any serious political voice in the ANC. The documents of the various conferences of the Women's Section reveal how hard women activists tried to win some measure of control over their programmes and some degree of authoritative voice in overall ANC decision-making. The 1981 conference of the Women's Section identified the key task as the mobilisation of women inside South Africa as active ANC members. The conference recommended that the head of the Women's Section should automatically become a member of the NEC. This would give women representation in the movement's highest decision-making body for the first time. Although the NEC accepted the proposal, an attempt was made in 1983 to overturn it on the grounds that the NEC was not a federal body and that women on the NEC were elected in their own right rather than as representatives of constituencies. The NEC's position was that the head of the Women's Section, Gertrude Shope, was 'in the NEC in her own right ... but she has every right to raise matters that affect the Women's Section. She has no obligation to report to the Women's Section on her work in the NEC.'

After the 1981 conference the Women's Section began to pay much greater attention to the importance of political education for its members and of providing more effective leadership to the emerging internal women's organisations. Mavis Nhlapo said that 'we saw the need to develop a theoretical basis for women's struggle'. Inspired by their travels to socialist countries and their exposure to different women's movements in Europe, younger women in the ANC began to think about developing a mobilising framework appropriate to South African women. They tried to strengthen the *Voice of Women* and to produce shorts on women's issues for the ANC radio station. Several units started internal education projects, broadening the previous focus on literacy and adult education to include education about women's political history and debates about the role of women in the liberation struggle. The Women's Section worked incredibly hard to raise funds and gather materials for the movement, especially clothing for women and children. In 1983 the Women's Secretariat also discussed the need for the movement as a whole to take responsibility for political education about the emancipation of women.

At this meeting some women expressed concern at the low number of women deployed as underground agents inside South Africa, with some arguing that this made it more difficult to mobilise women into the ANC and MK. The NEC never adequately addressed the problem and continued to treat women as a relatively minor constituency within the ANC.

The Women's Section's networks with women's organisations around the world, particularly the affiliates of the Women's International Democratic Federation, produced large amounts of money, clothing and equipment for the movement. Nevertheless, 'when we needed to finance women's projects, the treasurer-general would tell us there was no money for women,' Nhlapo said. At the same time the treasurer-general's office was not always meticulous about recording money that came in and informing the Women's Section of its arrival. At times this put the Women's Section in a difficult position with regard to donors, as the women were unable to account for specific donations.

Despite women's increasing visibility and role within the ANC in the early 1980s, the organisation continued to be male-dominated. At a 1982 seminar a speaker noted that 'men seem to want us to be perpetually in the kitchen. Our relations with them are jeopardised if we attend first to the non-domestic affairs and are late or unable to perform to perfection the domestic work that awaits us … Some men refuse to accept the leadership and authority of women, i.e. it would appear they support that the lady comrade is senior to them in authority but in practice they would never take her instructions.' Mtintso said that 'in some ways the organisation was also closed off. In raising women's issues we were seen as petty. We were called umzane – the women, while men were called the soldiers. There were already expectations of failure, so we have to overperform. Even men overperform in order not to be beaten by women. In that environment you can't raise gender issues – we are all laying down our lives. We only discussed it insofar as there are specific needs for women. We were not talking about politics.' Nhlapo recalled that women were constantly accused of 'not understanding, not being sufficiently committed to national liberation, diverting the movement, being difficult'. And not only the men or the leadership were resistant to political discussions about woman's emancipation. The East Africa Region of the Women's Section, for example, found it difficult to discuss the 'woman question' in Dar es Salaam. 'We found that politically it was risky to introduce the concept of a "revolution within a revolution" to young, politically immature people … It was acknowledged that the majority of our women are more practically than intellectually orientated,' the regional section reported in 1981. 'Although they are involved in the fight against the fascist regime, we do not necessarily approach it from the same angle … [Women] cannot be forced into political discussion when they are faced with concrete problems like food and clothing for themselves and their children … With this analysis the Committee felt that we had to try our best to attend to the women's problems; we have to be practical and make them feel involved, not being lectured to.'

Nonetheless, as mobilisation of women inside the country intensified, the Women's Section began to feel the political pressure and urgency to provide political leadership and direction. Increasingly, women within the exiled movement began to develop a feminist voice. In 1983 Ray Simons produced an assessment of the internal situation in which she urged less 'ceremonial mobilisation and greater strategic direction'. One mechanism for focusing activists' energies on strategic areas of mobilisation, and to raise ideological debate on the role of different sectors and agents in the national liberation struggle, was to designate special themes for particular years.

1984 was devoted to accelerating the mobilisation of women. The Year of the Women Committee, appointed by the NEC, identified the objectives for 1984 as to pay tribute to 'the fighting women of our country and to increase their fighting ranks and make them assume their rightful role in the forefront of the struggle'. With regard to the Women's Section's internal mobilisation, the goals would be to create a single national women's body and to broaden women's organisation inside South Africa.

The focus on forming a national women's body inside

the country, preferably under the name of the Federation of South African Women, was paramount. This would consolidate the organisation of women and 'promote unity in the ranks of women opposed to apartheid and supportive of the ANC, and reactivate women activists at home'. The Women's Section reminded women activists that their key task remained that of national liberation and called on them to 'spare no effort in organizing women to become underground workers for the ANC, and to take part in the armed struggle to liberate our country from the grip of the fascist warmongers and their puppets'. The basis for unity would be the Women's Charter, adopted at the founding conference of the Federation of South African Women in 1954. The thirtieth anniversary would provide the impetus for the revival. The Women's Section Internal Sub-committee urged underground comrades to set up an ANC caucus in the federation 'to ensure that in all this activity the movement should have a direct hand in guiding the formation of a national women's organisation'. However, a national women's structure could not be imposed by fiat from exile. Internal women's organisations were not ready for unity, and, despite numerous efforts well into the late 1980s, the revived Federation of South African Women did not gain a national presence.

The gap between the expectations of the exiled movement and the internal movement was starkly revealed in this case: the desire of the Women's Section for a strong sectoral representative body of women was out of kilter with the internal direction of the United Women's Organisation in the Western Cape, which was moving toward a strong grassroots body. The Women's Section was also out of step with the difficulties that the Natal Organisation of Women was facing in opposition from Inkatha and the state, and with the lack of organisational depth in the Federation of Transvaal Women. Although the Women's Section no doubt gave courage and legitimacy to its underground activists, its role in stimulating and directing the internal women's movement was limited by local concerns and power struggles.

The influence of the Year of the Women on official discourses within the ANC was much more visible even though – or perhaps because – there was no coherent programme of action. The Year of the Women exposed the ANC's weaknesses in integrating gender equality into the core work of the movement. Despite the creation of an organisation-wide committee to oversee the programme of action for the Year of the Women, it soon became the responsibility of the Women's Section rather than the movement as a whole. Nhlapo said that the Year of the Women failed in its most crucial task, that of 'making the women's issue a national issue and not just a women's issue'. In early 1984 the Women's Section began calling for more discussion about the role of women in the ANC. At the first meeting of the National Women's

Executive Committee in April 1984, the leadership noted that 'the role of the Women's Section in the ANC is often misunderstood by the membership' and called for a sustained programme of political education. Concerns were also raised about the degree of control that the Women's Section had over decision-making. The Women's Section repeatedly requested greater autonomy, although it was prepared to concede broad policy decisions to the NEC. It complained that 'sometimes the women feel that some seriousness is not attached to matters raised by women whereas decisions and recommendations are made for the benefit and the enhancement of the work of our struggle as a whole'.

The tentative and somewhat oblique language in which these requests and complaints were raised reveals the lack of organisational receptivity in the NEC, which tended to blame the complaints on ignorance and lack of discipline. A report from just one meeting between women representatives and the NEC shows the nature of the reception that women faced. Women representatives reported that the NEC member Joe Nhlanhla's concern was that 'one of our problems is that we women have become women first then ANC'. Women were warned against 'sectarianism', with Josiah Jele, another NEC member, arguing that there was no need for women to have a special role in decision-making 'because the leadership considers recommendations made by women'. The men again emphasised the 'vertical structure' of the ANC.

The secretary-general, Alfred Nzo, was unhappy that 'an impression of gross crime is being committed. The way the ANC regards women in the organisation, it is an ANC he does not [know] of ... He shared the views of the other comrades that there is no deliberate discrimination against women.' In a heavy-handed response the treasurer-general also dismissed the concerns raised by the National Women's Executive Committee, claiming that 'there are a lot of sentimental utterances about this and that ... if this meeting had a real programme of deliberation, he [the treasurer-general] would be contributing fully.' It was Oliver Tambo who was able to shift the meeting from the haranguing and ridiculing tone adopted by other members of the NEC to an emphasis on the importance of finding out what gave rise to women's unhappiness. Without the space Tambo created, the antagonistic response from the NEC might have ended women's attempts to transform the internal culture of the movement.

Undeterred, women activists continued to raise the 'woman question' and to push for a sharper understanding of the relationship between national liberation and women's emancipation, with the South African Communist Party journal *African Communist* providing an important forum for these debates. In 1984 an article by the pseudonymous Mosadi wa Sechaba located the urgency to organise women in the need to 'activate the masses' for the revolution and quoted Lenin's comment to Clara Zetkin that 'if the women are not with us, the counter-revolutionaries may succeed in setting them against us'. Understanding women's oppression as caused primarily by apartheid, the article posited a two-stage struggle in which women's emancipation would follow from national liberation.

Sechaba argued that 'women should be mobilised by making them realize that our national democratic revolution will free them not only from national oppression and class exploitation, but also from oppression as women. This will give them an extra motivation for joining the struggle. Women should be made aware that they are expected to contribute at every level in every trench of our struggle – in the military as well as the mass political struggle – and not as mere supporters and sympathisers.'

In 1985 the Women's Section called for a regional seminar to discuss the role of women in the struggle and within the ANC. The second ANC National Consultative Conference in Kabwe in June 1985 devoted a special session to women. A discussion paper circulated for the conference raised openly, for the first time, the collusion of men in the ANC with 'traditional, conservative and primitive constraints imposed on women by man-dominated structures within our movement. Our movement has the task, as a vanguard of the liberation struggle, of minimising these constraints as much as possible.' Arguing that 'in our beleaguered country the women's place is in the battlefront of struggle', the discussion paper boldly declared that 'our task is to prepare men and women for equality; this means that we must fight against male chauvinism, male domination, we must do away with male domination in the home, village, town, factory, workshop, in politics, economics and religion. In particular, we must fight domination even within our movement. No society is free if women are not free.' Bravely, considering the kind of reaction the Women's Section had faced in its meeting with the NEC in 1984, the paper again challenged the movement's tendency to belittle the work of the Women's Section and to see women as secondary subjects. It argued that 'a women's movement is as decisive as the imperativeness of a working class movement'.

These arguments finally began to gain support in the NEC. At Kabwe the NEC departed from its earlier approach of mobilising women solely for national liberation and formally recognised that women's equality would deepen and enhance the quality of democracy itself. The conference agreed that 'the task of organising and mobilising our women into a powerful, united, active force for the most thorough-going democratic revolution falls on men and women alike'. For the first time the Women's Section expressed an interest in a more thorough bill of rights, one that would reflect women's demands for equality, 'so that women know what they are fighting for'.

Oliver Tambo's closing speech as president at the conference was regarded as an affirmation of the need to strengthen women's voice within the ANC. Tambo advanced the proposition that South Africa should not be seen as free as long as women were oppressed and that women's oppression had to be addressed not just by women but by the movement as a whole. This marked the first of a number of significant declarations and statements by the ANC leadership aimed at providing political support for women's struggles to organise themselves. Tambo emphasised the need for women to be represented at all levels of the movement, including within the NEC. Later in 1985, at a meeting between the South West Africa People's Organisation (the Namibian liberation organisation) and the ANC in Kabwe, Sam Nujoma and Oliver Tambo made a joint pledge to the women of Namibia and South Africa that 'we would not consider our objectives achieved, our task completed or our struggle at an end until the women of Namibia and South Africa are fully liberated'. Tambo's role in supporting women's empowerment within the movement had a significant influence. His speech has since been quoted countless times in ANC debates dealing with the role of women.

The Nairobi Conference of the United Nations Decade for Women in July 1985 was a significant event for women in the ANC. It provided an opportunity for the Women's Section to meet directly with activists from home and to strategise about the strengthening of women's organisation. The Women's Section claimed to have secured unity between the United Women's Organisation and the Federation of South African Women during one of these meetings. Frene Ginwala has argued that the right-wing backlash at the conference inadvertently offered an opportunity for ANC women to take a leadership role. The United States delegation, led by Ronald Reagan's daughter Maureen, opposed a resolution against apartheid on the ground that this was a political issue rather than a women's issue. Issues like violence against women were posed as genuine women's issues, and the US delegation pushed hard (on the ground of feminism) for the exclusion of geopolitical issues from the conference resolution. The Women's Section had been alerted to this strategy well in advance by the NEC and had begun to prepare a position against it as early as 1984. It argued that 'there is a move to depoliticise the Nairobi Conference by the Zionist and pro-American element. They argue that if we talk politics, we cannot talk about actual development problems.'

The ANC delegation, fresh from a Non-Aligned Movement meeting in Delhi in April at which it had been agreed that growth, development and equity were intertwined, led the opposition to the US position. The ANC sent all its key women leaders to Nairobi, including Ruth Mompati, Frene Ginwala and Gertrude Shope, with the male leadership also present because the ANC had heard that South African President P.W. Botha was planning an international 'comeback' in Nairobi. Through its participation in the Non-Aligned Movement, the ANC delegation could draw on the support of the Latin American countries and India for a resolution against apartheid. Ginwala has said that this marked a turning point not only in the international struggle against apartheid but also in the debate about the relationship between the liberation of women and national liberation. At Nairobi the struggle was to reassert the ANC's stance that there could be no women's liberation without national liberation; in other words, the ANC fought against an apolitical feminism, which the American women seemed to represent, and asserted a socialist feminist position.

The experiences of women in Africa in the 1980s were especially influential in alerting women in the ANC to the need to formulate more effective strategies to integrate gender equality into the ANC's core principles. The post-liberation record of nationalist movements in most African countries was poor: women's position did not significantly improve after independence, despite rhetorical commitments by political leaders. The underlying structural forces that produced unequal relations of gender persisted and were in fact exacerbated by the lack of a systematic approach to the 'woman question'. The pattern that women activists discerned was that the focus during the liberation period of drawing women into active politics was dropped and in its place were allowed to re-emerge dominant ideological constructions of women's position as subordinate to men. These issues were highlighted at the first World Conference on Women in Mexico City in 1980, and especially at the UN Decade for Women meeting in Nairobi in 1985 at which the ANC Women's Section was highly vocal. This acute dilemma of nationalism – that women were promised fundamental transformation during the era of opposition struggle but sidelined when liberation movements took power – did not go unnoticed by South African women activists.

The experiences of other African countries also sounded warning bells within women's organisations inside South Africa. Intense debates had already begun in the mid-1980s on the relevance of feminism to national liberation as women's bodies began to delineate political spaces that were to some extent independent of the ANC. Yet women activists were articulating only in muted tones their growing reservations about the dominance of nationalist frameworks. For many women in the exiled movement, the brand of liberal feminism articulated by the official US delegation to the Nairobi Conference simply underscored their own criticisms of feminism as bourgeois, imperialist and irrelevant to the South African women's movement. Attitudes against feminism within the ANC and its allies hardened, even as women inside the movement were increasingly demanding a stronger political voice and greater autonomy in strategic decision-making related to the direction of the women's movement.

At the second conference of the ANC Women's Section, held in September 1987 in Angola, debates about the role of women in the movement between younger and older women, and between MK and the Women's Section, were dominant. The 'unity of women' in the ANC was visibly fractured. It was at this conference that the struggles described in this chapter for a greater role for women within the ANC and MK, the hankering for closer organisational links between women inside the country and in exile, and the demands for some degree of autonomy for women to define and articulate their interests and express these through a stronger organisational form, finally came together. The relationship between national liberation and women's liberation was put firmly on the agenda of the conference, seemingly against the wishes of older members of the Women's Section. A paper circulated before the conference, 'Women's Role in the NDR [national democratic revolution]', urged the movement to build women's emancipation into the project of 'people's power' and to accelerate the political participation of women. This position was supported strategically by introducing, through a tape-recording, a paper written by internal activists. The paper challenged the ANC Women's Section to get the ANC to state unequivocally its 'long term programme, strategy and tactics … in confronting women's oppression and safeguarding women's democratic rights in a free and united South Africa'. It raised again the lack of an independent constitution for the Women's Section and suggested that the ANC finally adopt a bill of rights 'which will be a document adopted by the ANC as a whole and not by women alone. This act will commit even more all the sectors of the ANC to the eradication of discrimination against women and the safeguarding of their rights in a free South Africa'. The Women's Congress of the United Democratic Front (UDF) encouraged the efforts of the Women's Section in its message of solidarity, urging the conference 'to correctly chart the way forward and prepare not only for the seizure of political power but for the strategic role of the women in a free and democratic and non-sexist South Africa'.

The participation and representation of women were seen as vital in ensuring that the conference address that equality. Delegates constantly made reference to the danger that the ANC's commitment to women's emancipation might degenerate into lip-service from the president and other leaders, with little attempt to address the need for implementation and action. In a paper entitled 'An Understanding of South African Women in Society and Their Role in the Liberation Struggle', one group of delegates pointed out that, while women participated in large numbers in grassroots organisations, 'they are glaringly absent at the leadership level. Are the two connected and, if so, how? Why is it that outside of women's organisations, and to some extent the trade unions, over 50% of the oppressed population has scant representation in the leadership of our struggle?' The paper outlined a range of factors that produced this outcome, including reluctance among both men and women to believe that women could be effective leaders. A paper prepared by women in MK suggested that at least some attention needed to be paid to the role and strength of the Women's Section itself. In its composite report the National Preparatory Committee commented that a gulf seemed to exist between the Women's Section and women in the military, with the Women's Section playing almost no role in providing political direction to women cadres. Visits by the Women's Section to the MK camps tended to focus on the immediate social welfare needs of women cadres, rather than on the strategic issues of the role that women cadres could play if deployed inside South Africa. The Women's Section 'is not a fighting organ. There seems to be a Chinese wall between the Women's Section and the Politico/Military Structures.'

Despite formal statements about the need for more women in leadership, women continued to be under-represented within political ANC structures. Ruth Mompati, a member of the NEC in the 1960s and again in 1985, highlighted the need for women to be organised within the ANC. 'Even in an organisation that supports the liberation of women, we have had to work hard to build the confidence of our women, because we are victims of history, victims of our traditions, victims of our role in society.'

The debate about the need for greater representation of women, raised initially at the Kabwe Conference but not followed through by the NEC, was again hotly debated at the ANC Women's Section conference in Lusaka in 1986. Members argued that if women were to be effectively organised inside the country, women within the ANC had to have a greater role in identifying women's problems and be 'involved in the solutions at all levels including the highest organs of decision-making'.

They questioned whether even sympathetic men could move beyond an 'intellectual perception' of women's oppression to act as effective representatives of women. The question of what representation would mean evoked different responses. For some activists the absence of women in leadership positions had consequences for the extent to which the norms and values of gender equality were institutionalised within the movement. An unattributed internal document commented that women had always been marginal to the work of the movement and that women's participation had not led to a 'challenge to men about women's subordination, within the ANC, and in society in general'. From this point of view participation had to be strengthened by greater representation. Others questioned whether representation per se would have an effect on the movement. For example, for Ruth Mompati, one of only three women (out of thirty-five) on the ANC's National Executive Committee in the late 1980s, women's under-representation on the ANC's internal structures was not a useful indicator of its attitude toward women. 'One of the reasons there are only three women on it is that very few senior women have left the country. But also there are a lot of women leaders inside the country who, if we had a free South Africa, would be on the National Executive. So we can't really judge the representation of women in leadership positions by looking at the National Executive of the ANC. Secondly, we have to continue to fight to put our women into leadership positions and to make them more able so that they can lead and articulate their problems.'

As Mompati's comment suggests, while calling for greater numerical representation of women on the NEC, the Women's Section was nevertheless concerned about the quality of representation. At the 1987 Women's Section conference a call for the implementation of the ANC's policy on equality was accompanied by a warning that transformation 'cannot be effected by simply appointing a few women to positions of leadership, or providing special training courses to help them overcome initial disadvantages'. Rather, what was needed was political education that challenged 'traditional patriarchal attitudes [which] not only prevent women joining the struggle, but affect those women already in the movement and prevent them contributing to their full potential'. The emphasis on the need for political education for men and women signalled the increasing extent to which women were articulating internal gender-based tensions within the movement. Male attitudes towards women – as 'backward, conservative and chauvinistic' – began to emerge explicitly as a problem in the organisation. MK activists described these as 'a cancer that is slowly but surely eating through the ranks of our organization ... The longer we nurse them like a terminal tumour, the deadlier they become both to ourselves and to the movement.' Male resistance to women's progress, once discussed tentatively, and qualified by statements reiterating the primacy of national liberation, was discussed openly and frankly in 1987. As women in MK wrote, 'At this moment in time we cannot afford the luxury of polite niceties.'

The concern about gender equality as political rhetoric was well founded. In 1988 the ANC issued its 'Constitutional Guidelines for a Democratic South Africa', 'widely regarded as the most important political document since the Freedom Charter,' according to Catherine Albertyn. In a careful analysis of the formulation of the guidelines, Dorothy Driver has argued that they 'did not meet the requirements posed by ANC feminists', despite revisions following a meeting between the Women's Section and the drafting committee. The guidelines acknowledged the need for gender equality in the public and private spheres and supported affirmative action as the means to effect equality.

However, this clause was the sole reference to gender equality. As Albertyn has pointed out, the guidelines' provisions 'refer to material inequality on the basis of race only'. Although the guidelines appear to incorporate the demands of women, 'the wording and location of the clause demonstrate little appreciation of the material and ideological underpinnings of gender oppression and provide little on which to base political and legal claims for substantive gender equality'. One key area of contention was the wording of the clause on the family. In its original formulation the clause provided for the 'protection of the family'. Dorothy Driver has noted that the ANC's National Executive Committee proposed a reconsideration of that clause, calling instead for 'the establishment of women's rights over their own fertility, and for childcare to be equally shared by fathers and mothers. Furthermore, it proposed the removal of patriarchal rights over the family.' The revised guidelines did not take these proposals into account. Instead, they were to appear in a separate charter of gender rights, to 'be incorporated into the Constitution guaranteeing equal rights between men and women in all spheres of public and private life and requiring the state and social institutions to take affirmative action to eliminate inequalities, discrimination, and abusive behaviour based on gender'. Lulu Gwagwa has noted that the clause in the guidelines on women reveals 'flaws in the ANC/MDM treatment of the family'. The ANC's political statements, she suggests, portray the body as having a static view of this dynamic organisation. This flaw originated from its use of the family as a mobilising tool, as a result of which power relations within the family are not examined. Instead, 'The family gets subsumed within the wider struggle against apartheid and capitalism.' Despite the enormous leaps in the understanding of equality within the ANC, the movement remained wedded to gendered assumptions about social roles.

The limitations of the guidelines highlighted the hurdles that still existed inside the ANC: the limitations for women of a movement driven primarily by a nationalist struggle and discourse. Writing about this period, Frene Ginwala notes the 'failure of the organisation to take its own policy on gender issues seriously'. She writes that the adoption of policies on gender equality 'owed more to the persuasive advocacy of some women members than to the level of understanding of either the membership or the entire leadership'. The shallowness of the commitment to gender equality had consequences for the extent to which women's demands might be institutionalised in the new democracy. As Driver has pointed out, 'A constitution cannot maintain itself without broad-based political support, nor can it in itself guarantee change.'

The struggles between women and men in the ANC, and between women within the Women's Section, did ultimately shift the ANC's position on the role of women in the movement. In August 1989 the ANC Women's Section in London held a seminar on 'Feminism and National Liberation', at which, for perhaps the first time, feminism was explicitly used as a legitimate language in which to describe women's struggles. Out of this seminar and related discussions in which both women and men participated, the ANC produced the 2 May 1990 document on 'the emancipation of women in South Africa'. This document recognised the need for the ANC to explicitly address the 'question of the emancipation of women', noting that the establishment of principles and the development of practices consistent with gender equality were 'long overdue'. The statement explicitly advocated affirmative action mechanisms and made responsibility for achieving gender equality one for the organisation as a whole, not just for women within it. The commitment was an important one. As Jacklyn Cock has noted, 'It means we are not some tiny marginalised group working for an eccentric goal. We have the support of a mass-based movement which not only shares our goals but which provides us with the space to formulate demands.'

The timing of the statement was also important as it signalled a promise by the ANC to carry its commitments into the democratic era and, by implication, into government. It opened a larger space for women – indeed, demanded of them – to begin to consider the concrete substance of their demands for equality in relation to key areas of social and legal policy-making. As a result lively and open debates on gender issues emerged during a range of conferences in the early 1990s.

Most notable among these discussions was the Malibongwe Conference, organised by the ANC and held in Amsterdam early in 1990, which brought together for the first time women in exile and activists inside South Africa – a mere two weeks before the unbanning of the ANC, PAC and SACP. This conference was a watershed event, not only because it brought women together but also because it addressed a range of issues – from the future democratic constitution and the political participation of women in political positions to violence, health care and customary law – in ways that prefigured gender debates about the constitution and about policy during the transition to democracy. For example, in a keynote address the senior ANC official Frene Ginwala (later co-convener of the Women's National Coalition) called for a post-apartheid constitution to include in its preamble a clause explaining gender oppression and its effect; to include an equality clause and place a constitutional duty on the state to ensure race and gender equality; to protect women from cultural practices that discriminated against them; and to recognise reproductive rights. This speech signalled a decisive break from the argument that demands for gender equality would divide and weaken the struggle against apartheid. The more explicit use of feminist language to frame women's demands was also evident in other papers, including those prepared by women's organisations inside the country. Although the theoretical formulations of gender remained relatively weak, the Malibongwe Conference reopened the possibility of feminism as an open political, and not merely academic, discourse.

7

The homecoming

On 2 February 1990, the National Party government lifted the bans on proscribed organisations, changing the landscape of politics in South Africa. To some extent the lifting of bans was a surprise to women activists. Although it came barely a week after the ANC's Malibongwe Conference in Amsterdam, at which the focus was squarely on women's visions and policy demands in post-apartheid South Africa, the implications of the unbanning for the autonomy of internal women's organisations were quite unforeseen.

Partly because of the energy generated at the Malibongwe Conference, women in the ANC immediately debated the implications of the unbanning. In May 1990 the ANC Women's League met in Lusaka with approximately seventy women from women's bodies inside South Africa to discuss the 'disbanding of current organisations and the possibility of their joining the ANC Women's League'. Despite the emphasis on the need for women's emancipation to be recognised as part of ANC policy, reflecting the momentum developed at Malibongwe, the meeting nevertheless resolved that 'the initial thrust of the Organisation would be to recruit members into the ANC. Thereafter women would be recruited into the League.' At the same time, 'much discussion revolved around empowering women, increasing their participation at all levels of the movement and especially in decision-making and policy formulation'. Those present agreed on a number of amendments to be proposed for the ANC constitution, then under discussion by the movement as a whole. These included the requirement that 'the ANC be responsible for the emancipation of women' and the need for developing enforcement mechanisms 'relating to gender relations, political rights, women workers' rights, harassment and abuse'. The meeting also agreed to recommend an amendment to the ANC constitution that would require that 25 to 30 per cent of National Executive Committee members be women. The meeting emphasised that the affirmative action programme should be 'not only position oriented but also task oriented'.

Along with other ANC substructures, the Women's Section returned to the country on a wave of triumphalism. The Women's Section reverted to the name of the ANC Women's League. The strategic emphasis agreed to in Lusaka, on mobilising women into the ANC rather than the league, was not unanimously supported in the league, with many activists wanting to retain a focus on women's liberation. However, this shift that they desired, from 'side by side' to feminism, was not easily achievable either. At a press conference in August 1990 in Durban to celebrate the return of the league, the more militant group within the league (Mavivi Myakayaka-Manzini, Baleka Mbete-Kgositsile and Frene Ginwala) emphasised the need to organise and mobilise women in defence of their rights. At the subsequent rally, however, a reporter found that 'it was hard to say what made it a women's rally. There were men speakers encouraging women, some men performers entertaining the crowd, lots of ANC fashion clothes, drum majorettes and women doing their usual thing – cooking. Selling all sorts of delicacies cunningly produced with a minimum of space and equipment at the side of the road. There was little vision for the future role of women – perhaps this was the task of the women delegates who met the day before – but there was lots of good cheer and comraderie [sic].'

But the league did not return to a political vacuum. During the years of exile, women's organisations had been formed in many parts of the country. The most important of these were the Natal Organisation of Women, the United Women's Congress in the Western Cape, the Federation of Transvaal Women and the Port Elizabeth Women's Congress. These were organisations rooted in community politics and they formed the backbone of the civic activism that was to develop into the United Democratic Front (UDF). Perforce, given the banning of the ANC, they had developed independently of the exiled movement. They had different modes of operation and organisational cultures, had experimented with non-hierarchical feminist styles of work, and were animated not only by opposition to apartheid but also by a determination to challenge patriarchy. There were strong women leaders in all these organisations, and while they may have shared political affinities with the ANC, they were by no means an internal arm of the league. Indeed, as I have shown, the league was generally out of touch with the campaigns and debates taking place in the country.

The re-establishment of the Women's League in South Africa was accompanied by intense debate about whether the internal women's organisations should retain some autonomy from the league. An over-riding issue was the capacity to sustain independence in the face of the transition to democracy. Since the mid-1980s women's organisations had been struggling to carve out an independent space from the UDF – unsuccessfully, as the urgency of national politics and the states of emergency swept everyone into crisis mode. Maintaining two women's organisations – an ANC Women's League as well as an independent women's grouping – in each region with similar aims and led by the same group of activists would be even harder. At the same time women activists needed to feel that they were part of a larger movement on the threshold of victory. The tension, as always, lay in the relationship between women's struggles and national struggles. Opportunistic or not, the dominance of the ANC Women's League was achieved surprisingly easily. At the meeting at which the United Women's Congress decided to dissolve, the MK soldier and trade unionist Lucy Nyembe said bluntly, 'The ANC must become the political home of women in this country. Our major task is to go into our communities and to organise in such a way that we draw women nearer to the ANC.' Thenjiwe Mtintso characterised the ANC position to integrate all women's organisations as 'opportunistic. The ANC wanted women to organise but within the ANC … Women's role within the ANC was to organise other women into the movement.'

Very quickly, a power struggle began to emerge between internal activists and exiles. 'Some women in leadership worried about whether in the ANCWL they would have the same power. Women, just like men, want power,' Phumelele Ntombela-Nzimande said. Tensions were strong around issues of control as well as of political capacity between the former exiles and members of the internal organisations. Some internal activists, such as Nozizwe Madlala-Routledge, felt that the returning exile leadership assumed that the exiles were in charge. 'We were disappointed with their attitude … We made several approaches, said we were ready to join, to assist. We were excluded, we felt deliberately.'

Whereas internal leaders had strong links to the grass roots and were well known, exiles had yet to prove themselves as individuals. Ntombela-Nzimande said, 'We didn't know Baleka [Mbete-Kgositsile], for example, from a bar of soap. Exiled women had their own challenges of getting credibility with those who had been inside and borne the brunt of repression.' An ANC cadre commented on her frustration on returning home: 'When I went outside, they saw you as part of the inside, and when we came back, we were seen as part of the outside.'

Although the exiles had vast international experience and were very aware of the international women's movement, they had little actual experience of building women's organisations, particularly under the difficult conditions that existed in many parts of the country (e.g. the violence in Natal). One activist commented that this limited their contribution. 'I was personally disappointed about the lack of vision of the ANCWL ... It was because of their role in exile. They were doing soft support work for the ANC. Inside we had a better, more realistic vision. It was us who raised the possibility at Malibongwe of the ANC being unbanned and the need to be prepared. They didn't raise it. The ANCWL put too much emphasis on petty issues, on personalities. They were antagonistic to strong women inside.' Jenny Schreiner also pointed out that exiled members of the Women's League had very little experience in building grassroots organisations and lacked the skills to take the league into the transitional period.

Nozizwe Madlala-Routledge noted that one weakness that emerged was 'the lack of a programme of action emerging from women's own articulation of their needs and agendas. We'd learned the value of this [in the Natal Organisation of Women].' While the Women's League was adamant about the political need to draw all women's organisations under its banner, inside the country there was a varied response to the issue of disbanding the independent internal women's movements. The majority of bodies linked to the UDF opted to fold their structures into the ANC Women's League. In the Western Cape and the Transvaal the decision to merge with the league was more easily taken than in Natal; it was seen as a fait accompli, an extension of the process of becoming a UDF structure. In a letter to the UDF, the United Women's Congress (UWCO) outlined its reasons for disbanding: '[The] Western Cape women's organisations followed in the footsteps of the ANC Women's League, and took up the spear when the ANC was in the underground. With the unbanning of the African National Congress, UWCO started a process of discussing our role in the new situation. UWCO decided that the role our organisation has played can now best be taken up again by the ANC Women's League. So UWCO will disband ... Our members are joining the ANC and working actively to build the Women's League. We are excited to be reunited with our comrades from exile, and to be part of the one national women's organisation, where our hearts and loyalties belong.'

It was, surprisingly, within the Natal Organisation of Women (NOW) that the strongest opposition to disbanding was expressed. NOW was divided into two camps on the issue of integration. One camp argued that NOW had existed as a women's formation under the banner of the UDF, itself aligned in vision, if not formally, with the ANC. The integration of NOW and the league was therefore a logical development. Another camp argued strongly for a women's organisation that was not politically aligned. For some women this was tied to the demand for a politically autonomous women's movement, in which women's struggles would be in alliance with, but not subordinated to, the national liberation movement. For many women in this camp, however, the issue was the safety of women activists in Natal townships, because of the concern that being identified as a member of the league might be dangerous in the context of ongoing ANC–Inkatha tensions. NOW member Phumelele Ntombela-Nzimande pointed out that 'none of these discussions was necessarily based on what would be the best vehicle to raise sharply our interests as women'.

While there were some concerns about the need for separate women's organisations, problems of capacity tipped the balance in favour of disbanding – the same thin layer of women activists would have to work within both the league and an independent women's organisation. Furthermore, if relationships between exiles and internals were strained, they would be even more problematic if independent organisations continued to exist. Partly for this reason, one activist said, 'I felt we should disband because the antagonism shown by women in the ANCWL was too difficult for us to handle. We didn't have the capacity to function side by side. We had to close down because some women were involved in both the ANCWL and [the internal women's organisation]. The antagonism to the internals was untenable.'

But the dissolution process was not without its costs. A major step backward was a reinforcement of the shift away from the process of building a mass base. Jenny Schreiner, a member of the United Women's Congress, the Communist Party and the ANC, said, 'The decision to relaunch the Women's League was correct. All the UDF women's organisations were clearly ANC-aligned. But I'm not sure we should have disbanded organisations as quickly as we did. We lost the mass-based nature of women's organisations … We also lost the nonracialism. The first Women's League executive was very African. We lost the mass base, and I'm not sure we established a good balance between external and internal.'

Nozizwe Madlala-Routledge concurred: 'We pointed out [to the exiles] how hard we'd worked to build an alliance across class and race, and it was lost … treated as unimportant. The people brought in from the inside were

Winnie Mandela, et cetera – they were not representative of the women.' Fatima Meer has argued that while the disbanding of women's organisations 'strengthened the Women's League, at the same time it demobilised and weakened groups that had built grassroots support and carried out practical projects for many years.' The values of internal democracy and accountability that had characterised the UDF-affiliated bodies were underplayed in the power struggles for leadership of the national women's movement. 'Leadership had taken on a different meaning,' Madlala-Routledge said. 'It became a ticket to power, whereas during the 1980s the reward from being a leader was having support, that you were doing what members wanted you to do.'

The unbanning of the liberation movements in February 1990 posed new challenges for the ANC Women's Section – now reconstituted as the ANC Women's League – and for its relationship to both the ANC leadership and the internal women's movement. By the end of the 1980s women's organisations inside the country were fragile and vulnerable to the dictates of the male-led internal anti-apartheid movement. One consequence was that they were unable to effectively establish autonomy from the ANC Women's Section once it was unbanned, or to sustain an independent presence. And yet the transitional period demanded active political interventions to ensure that any future political negotiations and their outcomes, as well as future policies, were representative of and favourable to women. The challenge was who would lead the women's movement and whether the incipient feminism developed inside the country and in exile could translate into effective political action.

To facilitate the relaunch of the league on 9 August 1990, a task force was assembled, composed of ten women from the former ANC Women's Section and ten activists from inside the country, convened by Albertina Sisulu and Gertrude Shope. The primary role of the task force was to begin a recruitment drive. By December 1990 membership was estimated at 35,845, with 422 branches and 243 potential new branches. Initial problems identified included such logistical difficulties as lack of transportation and office facilities, and the structural difficulties in the relationship between the ANC and the Women's League in individual branches and regions.

Two key debates accompanied the relaunching of the league: the status of the league within the ANC, and the relationship between the league and UDF-affiliated women's organisations. With regard to the ANC's internal structure, the Women's League (and the Youth League) had no formal standing on the National Executive Committee, the movement's key decision-making structure. The ANC's position was that there was no need for the separate representation of women but rather that branches should ensure that their representatives included women. But the league argued that this ignored 'the fact that delegates come with mandates from their branches and thus not obliged to represent the league ... The league has as its major role the task of spearheading the emancipation of women within the ANC and the South African society in general ... There is therefore no way the task of the league can be ignored or taken for granted. It can also not be argued that this task can be fulfilled by any women who happen to attend conference ... Women members of the ANC will not automatically be members of the league.'

The ANC leadership agreed to allow the league 52 members to participate as full delegates to the ANC Consultative Conference to be held that year in Durban. Despite this victory, unresolved issues of representation left over from conferences in Kabwe and Lusaka recurred in the league: at a national consultative meeting of the league in Johannesburg in December 1990, members expressed concern about the lack of representation of women in the various working groups and structures of the movement. The conference resolved to call for the 'concrete implementation of the programme on affirmative action'.

These debates were more than procedural. The league that was reconstituted was significantly different from the structure that had been banned in 1960. By 1990 the old conception of the league as an auxiliary structure was under attack from within the Women's Section itself. Younger members of the new league were seeking greater reassurance that the ANC would indeed commit itself to women's emancipation once it came to power. The status of the reconstituted league would, in their view, symbolise the extent of the ANC's commitment. The Women's League task force argued that 'the ANCWL is a mass organisation of women within the ANC. It cannot be equated to a department. It has structures and membership which it has to represent and take care of.' Justifying the demand for the redefinition of roles and responsibilities of the league, Gertrude Shope, head of the ANC's Women's Section in exile, argued that 'we have never fought shy of committing ourselves to the struggle against national domination and racial oppression. Equally, we cannot afford to surrender our rights to end our oppression as women. How we define ourselves will determine how we relate to the ANC as a mother body.'

Under pressure to fulfil the promises of the 2 May document on the emancipation of women in South Africa, the National Executive Committee agreed to the launch of the league as 'an autonomous organisation able to make its own decisions in the struggle, within the overall policy of the ANC'. Frene Ginwala commented that 'for the first time the Women's League … is not a department or sub-section as it has been in the past … It will engage in its own decision-making within overall ANC policy, it will have its own funding, the right to own property, control bank accounts, in other words, the real mechanisms of power … The league is seen and sees itself as an autonomous body. It is not a federation of any kind, so other organisations can't affiliate to it. It is only open to ANC members. Women who are members of the ANC can join or not join, as they choose.'

To be effective within the ANC and strengthen its argument for greater autonomy, the league had to be seen to be leading a strong – and identifiable – constituency. However, the process of assuming leadership of the progressive women's movement was neither consistent nor entirely successful. Even at the early stage of unbanning, the Women's League recognised that there might well be a need for a broader alliance of women's organisations, even if all the UDF women's bodies dissolved into the ANC. In a reflection of the weaknesses of the Women's Section in building links with and mobilising women during the 1980s, it was clear that the league did not have dominance in the women's movement. At a crucial meeting between internal activists and the Women's Section in May 1990, those in attendance agreed that an alliance should be started, perhaps in 1991, in part to build relations with women who supported the UDF but not necessarily the ANC.

In April 1991 the ANC Women's League held its first national conference after its unbanning. The organisation met in Kimberley, where delegates elected the national executive of the Women's League. More than one thousand delegates from ANC Women's League branches and regions attended. Glenda Daniels has argued that the 1991 National Conference of the league 'underlined the recent shift towards a more assertive and possibly "feminist" Women's League which will take the specific oppression of women seriously'. The new executive board was a mix of older women activists and young feminists but was dominated by exiles.

Gertrude Shope, former leader of the Women's Section, was elected president and UDF member Albertina Sisulu was elected vice-president. Both Shope and Sisulu were sensitive to the concerns of younger women activists, recognising their importance in shaping the new direction of the league. Nevertheless, debates about the role of the league were heated, the options characterised by the independent feminist magazine *Speak* as 'mothers' club or fighting force'. Some members were comfortable with 'women's traditional role of bearing children and serving men. Others believe women must be liberated from all forms of exploitation and oppression if they are to be truly liberated.'

Media interviews with Shope reveal the extent to which the role of the league was unresolved even at the leadership level. On the one hand, Shope described the tasks in terms that resembled the old Women's Section's language of mobilisation. Invoking the discourse of motherhood, she argued that 'as women we brought life into this world and I don't see why we cannot do something to protect it'. She identified a common set of interests shared by all women, 'regardless of whether you are a woman in the northern suburbs or a mother in a township, the death of a child is a feeling that all women can understand. This instinct of a mother and a woman has to be a factor in bringing us together.' At the same time, however, Shope argued for the need to 'take a stand on women's emancipation'. She warned that support for the ANC in the negotiations was not 'at all costs', thereby signalling the growing feeling within the league that it would have to mobilise support for women's representation from non-ANC sources. However, Shope described the strategy for organising women as a gradual process: 'I am not saying that tomorrow we will not become radical, but we have to start somewhere. We don't want to start with something that is very drastic. We will ascend, step by step, so that once we have reached that peak, no one will question our action.'

The Kimberley conference debated the structure of the league at length. A key concern was to ensure that the leaders of the Women's League would be accountable to the grassroots membership and that branches would have power within the organisation. 'Women want more than democratic conferences,' *Speak* reported. 'They want democracy every day and they want their leadership to be accountable to them.' The problem with taking these commitments further was that the league had yet to establish itself as an organisation with members and mandates. As the secretary-general, Baleka Mbete-Kgositsile, wryly pointed out, 'What do you structure if you have no membership?' The pace of events internal to the league and in the negotiation process would make building organisation even more difficult than the leadership anticipated.

At the conference the Women's League was immediately plunged into a crisis regarding leadership issues. The central problem related to the role of Winnie Mandela, who ran against Gertrude Shope for the position of president. Shope was head of the ANC's Women's Section; Mandela was president of the league's powerful Pretoria-Witwatersrand-Vaal (PWV) region in the Transvaal. Mandela's profile as 'mother of the nation' and wife of Nelson Mandela gave her a unique symbolic claim to a leadership position in the Women's League. By this stage, however, she was on trial for kidnapping and assault in relation to the death of Stompie Seipei and the disappearance of Lolo Sono. In the Western Cape a branch of the Women's League threatened to break away if Mandela was elected. The Federation of Transvaal Women, whose core members were in the PWV region, was already divided on the issue of loyalty to Mandela, and some members voiced concerns at the Kimberley conference that she would not be an appropriate choice for president. Her position as the wife of the president of the ANC also worked against her; many feminists were concerned that the league would simply become another 'wives' club', like other leagues in Africa, thereby entrenching the auxiliary role. At the same time some members feared that Shope was both too 'old school' and 'soft' to provide the quality of leadership that would be required to carry the organisation through the difficult transition period.

Some considered Mandela's election bid to be part of a broader campaign on her part to strengthen her position in the ANC: as president of the league, she would automatically become a member of the ANC's National Executive Committee. Her reputation as a tough, even ruthless leader appeared to scare some delegates away from open opposition. One unnamed delegate told the *Star* newspaper that 'if there is a secret ballot, we hope Mrs Mandela will be outvoted. But if there is an open ballot, she will certainly be elected.' Indeed, electoral procedures were debated for hours at the conference to ensure that the decision would be respected. Shope defeated Mandela, winning 422 votes to Mandela's 196 in a secret ballot. The league proposed to draw up a leadership code for its officers that would give to members the right to recall leaders guilty of misconduct. While this had overtones of earlier attempts by the UDF to discipline Winnie Mandela, the proposal for a leadership code also signalled a larger concern with issues of accountability of leadership to membership. This was the first such proposal within the ANC.

For some these debates, while important, had the effect of distracting the league from deeper organisational issues. 'We didn't debate how we could become strong in the ANC and how to articulate our issues,' Ntombela-

Nzimande noted. 'We had women with extreme analytical tools and experience under one roof, but they were subsumed by the leadership debate. This weakened the ANCWL so that it has become just a shadow.' The new leadership did in fact identify a set of immediate tasks for the Women's League. These included programmes to address social and sexual oppression, the revival of the proposal to set up an ANC commission on emancipation, and the initiation of a charter of women's rights. The issue of the charter was an important one; it was a continuation of a process that had begun with the Kabwe discussions on a bill of rights in 1985 and had been identified as a priority during the planning for Kimberley. At this point, although the league sought to accommodate older 'motherists' as well as the younger and more assertive feminists who were emerging within the movement, the overall direction of the league confirmed a feminist direction.

Young women were determined that there would be no return to the league's role as an auxiliary structure and that the league had the potential to be the strategic base from which to seal the ANC's transformation into a movement that was fully committed to gender equality. Winnie Mandela's bid for leadership of the league did not end with her defeat at Kimberley. In 1993, at the second National Conference of the Women's League, she again stood for election to the presidency, this time successfully. Gisela Geisler has articulated the view of many young feminists, that this election 'effectively closed the Women's League's short history as a progressive women's voice'. Tensions between Mandela and the younger feminists grew as she was criticised for not taking the league or her position as president seriously enough. Some saw her as squandering the hard work that had been put into developing the league as an independent organisation. By 1995 she was being accused of using the league as a stepping-stone to personal power. The *Weekly Mail & Guardian* characterised her leadership style as autocratic and charged that she was using the league 'as a platform to launch attacks on the ANC'. Finally, in 1997 matters came to a head when eleven members of the executive and many rank-and-file members resigned from the league. Winnie Mandela, however, continued to lead the organisation and was re-elected at the National Conference in 1997, promising to lead members to 'the promised land'.

Within the ANC more broadly, women found that, despite the policy statement of 2 May 1990, there were many obstacles to the implementation of equality within the movement. In Kimberley, Oliver Tambo commented that 'the position of women within the democratic movement still leaves far too much to be desired … Condemned to menial tasks forever, rarely do they aspire or are seen as potential candidates for high office.' The league itself reminded its members that 'in the past year we have won many victories, which places us in the process of transition towards the building of a new South Africa. The women's movement has played an important role in making this present process possible. However, we have learnt from many countries that this does not automatically secure our liberation in a future SA.'

These organisational roadblocks – and the need for a much stronger women's organisation – were dramatically revealed at the 48th National Congress of the ANC, held in Durban in July 1991. This congress, the first since the unbanning, adopted a new constitution for the ANC, offering an opportunity for the Women's League to formalise women's representation in the organisation's decision-making structures. The Women's League decided before the conference to call for a quota of seats for women on the National Executive Committee (NEC) – an initial demand of 25 per cent was later revised to 30 per cent. At a preliminary inter-regional meeting to prepare for the congress, the Constitutional Committee, the outgoing NEC and all the regions accepted the proposal over a cumbersome alternative that would have included Women's League chairs and secretaries from each region on the NEC. At the conference, however, the Constitutional Committee proposed that the quota be dropped from the constitution. This provoked one of the most bitter and heated debates within the ANC since its unbanning.

Arguments against the quota included that election to the NEC should be on merit, that the system posed too many problems with regard to accountability, and that national liberation was the first priority. Debate was deadlocked. As Pat Horn has pointed out, given that only 17 per cent of conference delegates were women, using 'the tried and tested method of resolving issues by majority vote was in danger of perpetuating, rather than resolving this problem'.

The conference fell apart and, at the suggestion of Nelson Mandela, was adjourned to allow a meeting of the boards of the ANC, Women's League and Youth League to reach a compromise. The outcome of the process was disappointing: 'The following day, the President of the ANCWL apologised to the conference for the ANCWL's disruption of the vote and creating a delay the previous day, before a statement by the ANCWL was read out on the quota issue, proposing that the matter be finalised one way or the other. Unfortunately some delegates took this as an apology for having raised the quota issue at all, and one male delegate stood up and patronisingly rapped the women over the knuckles for the indignity which he blamed them for introducing into the conference by their tenacious fight and demonstration for the 30% quota. The 30% quota fell by the wayside.'

Women activists were angry at the outcome. Baleka Mbete-Kgositsile, secretary-general of the Women's League, said that women 'felt the NEC had abandoned them'. Several commentators also noted the strategic errors made by the league itself in the period leading up to the conference. Ginwala has pointed out that 'women members and the ANC Women's League also failed to engage the membership in debate prior to the conference or to promote and project the policies they wanted conference to adopt. In the months following the Women's League conference decision to put forward the quota proposal, its own activities focused almost exclusively on campaigns around issues such as the release of political prisoners, and the violence that was unleashed against the people with the connivance of the police and security forces. In practice the league functioned simply as an arm of the ANC, mobilising women into the organisation and the current national struggles. There was little in its approach or activities that was specific to women.' The league, she argued further, had 'failed its first test' and 'lent substance to those critics who have long argued that a woman's [*sic*] organisation attached to the ANC would inevitably subordinate women's interests'.

It was clear from the quota fiasco that the Women's League on its own would not be able to generate sufficient pressure on the ANC, let alone on other political parties, to address gender equality. For many women activists it was a valuable learning experience. 'It showed that women have to prepare, educate and organise at a grassroots level to pull off this kind of proposal,' one activist told *Speak*. 'It also proved that even when you are promised support from senior leadership, it doesn't mean that you will get it.' Kgositsile pointed out: 'We've got the future looking at us. We must plan workshops and we must put pressure on the national leadership to make sure that the new constitution ensures the emancipation of women. This is where the ANC Women's League's campaign for a charter for women's rights comes in.'

The nature of the defeat, rather than the substance of the quota debate, hardened women's resolve to develop a strong organisational base, even if this meant going outside the ANC. Kgositsile's comments indicated again the need for a national women's movement, a development that was to have a major influence on the constitutional negotiations. The forum for this debate was to emerge in the discussions that began in 1991 after the Women's National Coalition was formed.

Within the ANC a long-standing suggestion to form a commission on the emancipation of women, which would address the internal issues of women's representation in leadership and monitor the extent to which women's interests were reflected in policy-making, was finally acted on in February 1992. The commission was appointed to follow through on the demand made by women in 1987 and the NEC statement of 2 May 1990, and was perhaps a sop to women after the defeat of the quota proposal. It was headed by Oliver Tambo, with Frene Ginwala as his deputy. The terms of reference included examining, promoting and monitoring mechanisms for affirmative action within the ANC at all levels, ensuring that 'women's experiences and perceptions inform ANC strategy and tactics and its decisions at all levels', including policy, and promoting and undertaking research on gender. In its report to the ANC in December 1994, the Emancipation Commission highlighted the distance that the movement still had to travel before women were full and equal participants. It revealed that most women on the ANC payroll were secretaries, with little or no participation in decision-making. The adoption of the ANC's policies on gender equality by the branch and provincial structures was erratic and the importance of women's representation was mostly ignored by members.

While the commission on its own did not make major gains in overcoming these limitations, it provided an organisational space for Ginwala to advance the feminist activists' agenda in the ANC, separate from the troubled Women's League, and it formed the base from which the Women's National Coalition could be driven. Both the Emancipation Commission and the Women's National Coalition underscored the point that the league was not the only space in which women activists within the ANC could find a home.

The Women's National Coalition would play a decisive role in shaping the formal institutions of democracy. An equality clause was included in the Constitution after considerable debate over its wording, and the coalition successfully defended the idea that gender equality should trump the recognition of cultural rights.

8

Handmaidens of the party

Women took their place in the democratic parliament in no uncertain terms. Following the successful mobilisation of the Women's National Coalition and the victory over the insertion of an equality clause in the Constitution, the quota issue was reopened in the run-up to the first democratic elections in April 1994. This time around, the Women's League was successful in advancing the strategy, and a one-third reservation for women was accepted in both the national and provincial lists. The result was that the new parliament had close to 30 per cent of women among its MPs, and the global image of South African democracy was much burnished by its presentation as women-friendly. For a time, the locus of gender politics shifted to the civil service and parliament, and there was significant optimism about what might be achieved with the right combination of political will and understanding about gender equality.

Several women MPs in the ANC – such as Pregs Govender, Lydia Kompe, Ellen Kuzwayo, Mittah Seperepere and Frene Ginwala – were determined to use their new positions in the legislature to advance the position of women. They had some allies in other parties as well, thanks to the collaborations built in the Women's National Coalition. However, most of the gender activists had come through the ranks of the internal women's organisations and their positions in the ANCWL were not strong. Several simply worked outside the league's structures. In parliament they formed the ANC Women's Caucus and strategised about how to get crucial pieces of legislation onto the party's agenda. This was a key pressure point for gender equality in the first democratic parliament and it effectively shaped the agenda of the multi-party Joint Monitoring Committee on the Improvement of Quality of Life and Status of Women (JMC). However, the insights and direction depended very much on the *nous* and vision of a small group of people led by Pregs Govender, whose work was crucial in the Workers' College, the training ground for trade unionists, and the Women's National Coalition, rather than the league per se. The committee was the only parliamentary structure to openly oppose the arms deal, but when Govender resigned from parliament in frustration at the end of 2002, her departure left a strategic vacuum. The league continued to control the agenda for equality in parliament, but without any real sense of direction.

Even in the very first years of democracy, there were signs that the ANCWL would be challenged by other women's organisations about the extent to which they represented the interests of poor women. An inkling of this could be discerned in the politics surrounding the redefinition and expansion of state support to the country's poorest children. The new government appointed a committee under the renowned academic Francie Lund, to design a new grant that would reach more children than the existing state maintenance grant, for which poor mothers were eligible. That grant had been taken up by poor Indian and Coloured mothers, white poverty having been virtually eliminated; while African mothers were not eligible. The Lund Committee had to balance the extension of the grant on a massive scale while at the same time ensuring that it would be fiscally sustainable. They recommended a grant at a level significantly lower than the old state maintenance grant, awarded directly to the child rather than to the mother. Protests against the lowered rate erupted, and were most marked in the Western Cape, where the New Women's Movement dominated.

The New Women's Movement was an organisation of ANC supporters who were disaffected by the ANC Women's League, claiming that it was elitist and out of touch with the interests of poor women. Most (but not all) of the constituency of the NWM were poor Coloured women who stood to lose substantially from the reduction in the amount of the grant. Although the NWM organised women on the basis of their class position, they were very quickly accused of being a Coloured women's organisation and their opposition to the child support grant was portrayed by the ANC Women's League as being anti-African. Tensions between the two movements, each claiming to represent poor women, were high enough that at least one protest turned into a violent confrontation between the two groups. That early harbinger of the ways in which differences in interest between women might shape political organisation did not lead to the development of any sustained alternative to the ANCWL or to the reinvention of the league inside the ANC. Instead, its rightward drift continued, and the space of opposition and new thinking about gender inequality shifted to the NGO sector, and particularly to those organisations that were dealing with rising levels of violence against women.

On another crucial legislative front, related to the passage of the Domestic Violence Act, the league was (to borrow a phrase by Sheila Meintjes) 'conspicuously ineffective'. Alliances between the organisations in the violence against women sector and interventions by feminist lawyers were much more significant in getting the legislation passed in 1999.

Inside the state, the Women's League began playing an active – and, some argue, gatekeeping – role in ensuring that ANC women were appointed to positions in parliamentary committees and government departments, as well as to the parastatal institutions and oversight bodies. The Commission for Gender Equality (CGE), designed to be a mechanism for accountability independent from political parties and assured wide powers by the Constitution, was one casualty of the emerging politics of patronage. To some extent, the feistiness of parliamentarians such as Pregs Govender had an impact on appointments to the CGE, as it became more important politically to ensure that the CGE would not take on the government. There were some calls for the CGE, to address issues such as the provision of treatment to women with HIV and AIDS, as well as to take on a campaign against sexual violence – both agendas that revealed massive problems in Thabo Mbeki's reign as president. The CGE steered clear of such controversies, eventually becoming so mired in its own organisational dysfunctionalities that it became virtually moribund.

The league also controlled the Office on the Status of Women (OSW), located in the Presidency, which had overall responsibility for the mainstreaming of gender equality across all government department policies and programmes. Lack of resources, institutional resistance and, not least, the reluctance of the leadership in the OSW to openly challenge the ruling party undermined the effectiveness of the government machinery. Appointments to both the CGE and the OSW seem to have been driven by considerations of party loyalty and political mobility rather than by a track record in gender activism or expertise in the frameworks of feminism.

Even when the league was faced with the fate of its own comrades – such as the rape of Nomboniso Gasa on Robben Island, and the abuse of the league stalwart Mavivi Myakayaka-Manzini by her husband (himself a senior ANC figure) – the league refused to take positions that might pit it against the party leadership. When the ANC Women's Caucus called in parliament for further measures to be instituted to protect the women in these situations, they were firmly dissuaded from doing so by the ANC Women's League.

Although most forms of unfair legal discrimination against women were removed in the first parliamentary term of the democracy, various laws were subsequently introduced by the ANC that troubled feminists and that the ANCWL seemed either powerless or unwilling to stop. In 2003 and 2004 two key legislative interventions appeared to show either a conservative turn in the ANC or a more concerted attempt to woo traditional leaders at the expense of the rights of women. These were the Traditional Leadership and Governance Framework Bill, championed by the Portfolio Committee on Provincial and Local Government, and the Communal Land Rights Bill, sponsored by the Portfolio Committee on Land and Agriculture. The Communal Land Rights Act, enacted in 2004, aimed at ensuring security of tenure in rural areas. The Act provided for significant decision-making powers for traditional councils over the occupation, use and administration of communal land.

The troubling aspect for gender activists was whether rural women would be able to exercise their civil and political rights in relation to economic resources. The responsible Minister of Agriculture and Land Affairs was Thoko Didiza, a leading member of the league. The ANCWL was opposed to the Communal Land Rights Act, but was unable to prevent the party from pushing through the legislation. The Commission for Gender Equality eventually responded to the pressure from women's organisations and made a submission opposing the Act, a sign for many activists that a more independent Gender Equality Commission appeared to be emerging. The Joint Monitoring Committee pointed out that women would be a permanent minority on traditional councils, and requested that a quota of 50 per cent of seats be allocated. This was a rare occurrence of one portfolio committee challenging another. Yet there was little evidence that the presence of league members in parliament – a significant number in the ranks of ordinary MPs, as well as in Cabinet – would constitute an early-warning system when it came to setbacks to the equality clause. Some parliamentary insiders – tellingly, they did not wish to be quoted – argued that women MPs had instructions 'from above' not to oppose the Bill. The finalisation of the Bill and its appearance before the National Assembly occurred while party electoral lists were being drawn up, and some activists have suggested that women MPs feared that they might be left off or pushed low down on the lists. One ANC MP argued that 'it didn't appear to be an opportune time to take on the party'. Ironically, some of the very factors that had assisted women activists with regard to the Termination of Pregnancy Act – the role of senior members of the Cabinet and the portfolio committees and the 'party line' of the ANC – appeared to have worked against them. This has led one prominent feminist activist to question 'whether there is a strong anchor for gender activism in parliament any more. We have lots of women in parliament but I wonder how strongly they support women's interests when push comes to shove. Especially at election time the party is what matters.' The ANC Women's Caucus, which had been so effective in getting the controversial Termination of Pregnancy Act passed, did not take up the issue of rural women's rights in the Communal Land Rights Bill.

The Traditional Leadership Bill provided for 30 per cent representation of women in traditional councils. It also provided that, while 40 per cent of the members of the council were to be elected, the remaining 60 per cent 'must comprise traditional leaders and members of the traditional community selected by the principal traditional leaders concerned in terms of custom'. The bill also gave the Minister of Agriculture and Land Affairs discretionary powers to determine the nature and content of land rights, without requiring women's consultation or consent. This was in part a response to the concerns of women's organisations that gender equality issues might not automatically be taken into account, or might be over-ridden by the traditional councils. In these cases, the minister would be able to confer rights to ownership or occupation on women. These changes were far from satisfactory for traditional leaders, who saw them as further eroding their authorities.

The Communal Land Rights Act was ultimately struck down by the Constitutional Court in 2010, on the grounds of inadequate public participation during the process of formulation (and not on the grounds of the implications for rural black women of bolstering the power of traditional leaders).

The rift between women in government and 'ordinary' women widened under Mbeki's presidency on two core issues: women's economic position, and the relationship between sexualities and violence. It was perhaps an inevitable rift, given the massive opportunities that opened up for a small group of women as a result of the new affirmative action programmes. Feminism in the ANC became increasingly associated with Mbeki, who repeatedly articulated the need for women's representation in government during his presidency and appointed several women to his Cabinet. The politics of quotas and inclusion into the formal political sphere catapulted a few well-placed women into positions of influence and wealth. However, the evidence with respect to addressing the structural basis of gender inequalities is mixed, at best. Although poor women are the main claimants of the expanded social grants system – according to the 2011 census, over 11 million women claim the child support grant – poverty and unemployment are still disproportionately distributed by gender. Gender inequalities are compounded by poor economic growth and deep, inherited problems in the economic framework of the country, but despite an outward commitment to equality the ANC has not provided the political and theoretical leadership that might shape economic and social policies. The interventions of ANC women MPs in policy debates have been characterised by support for relatively conservative social attitudes that reinforce the view that women are primarily nurturing, caring members of a community rather than citizens with rights and entitlements to social and public resources.

The alignment of the demand for women's rights to a narrower project of numerical representation of women through quotas had political costs that became more apparent by 2009. One of the most significant was the loss of the demands for economic rights for poor women, which had been at the forefront of the Women's Charter for Effective Equality adopted by the Women's National Coalition in 1994. Although many advances were made under Mbeki's presidency in progress towards the equalisation of opportunities for women who were part of the political and economic elites, the complicities between the league leadership and the ANC Mbeki-ite faction annoyed many rank-and-file members of the ANC. It may even have set back popular support for feminism, as gender equality did not seem to be articulated in terms of redistribution of economic resources. The equality agenda became contrasted with a pro-poor agenda, rather than being allied with it.

In 2006 Phumzile Mlambo-Ngcuka, who replaced Jacob Zuma as Deputy President, was loudly booed at a Women's Day rally in KwaZulu-Natal in August. This was a stark demonstration of the extent to which the Mbeki-aligned faction in the ANC was losing support, and in the period leading up to the Polokwane contest for leadership the position of the league would become a central factor. Overt support for gender equality was seen as a proxy indicator of support for Mbeki and opposition to Jacob Zuma's candidacy. The league had a strategic choice facing it and, yet again, it stumbled by backing a candidate on the grounds of party power rather than on the extent to which he would support the league's avowed core values.

It could perhaps be argued that the league was merely following its rank-and-file members in throwing its weight behind Zuma. It is not surprising that so many women in the branches of the ANC supported Zuma: although, politically and legally, women have been the biggest winners of democratisation, they are also the key shock-absorbers of economic failures. Zuma supporters argued that under his presidency the control of the party would return to the branches and an agenda of economic redistribution would be foregrounded, and that this consideration was so important that the implications of his social conservatism and his problematic relationships with women should be set aside. It was a reprise of the arguments used to sideline feminists in the 1980s and 1990s.

In that context, the league could stand its ground on the importance of addressing the glaring gender inequalities, and either step outside the factionalised leadership struggle or offer up its own candidate. After all, for the first time in its history, the possibility of a woman standing for President was a serious consideration. Among the potential candidates were Nkosazana Dlamini-Zuma, Jacob Zuma's ex-wife and a political powerhouse in her own right, with deep roots in the league. Phumzile Mlambo-Ngcuka was another powerful candidate. It was the avowed position of the league that women should be in senior positions in the ANC and government, and in relation to the Zuma–Mbeki fight the league initially announced its intention to remain non-aligned. The ANCWL president, Nosiviwe Mapisa-Nqakula, stated that the league would be supporting a leader on a principled platform that would include the values of 'good principles, selflessness, cadreship and years of service to the movement'.

At the Polokwane conference in 2007, Mbeki strongly

mooted that the candidate to replace him should be a woman, and at the June 2007 policy conference he supported the Women's League's demand that the party should increase its quota for women on electoral lists from 33 per cent to 50 per cent. However, Mbeki's favour within the party had sunk so low that his support virtually doomed the debate. And the league opportunistically backed Mbeki's opposition for minor positions in government. Both Ncguka and Dlamini-Zuma would go on to occupy powerful positions outside the country – Dlamini-Zuma as the first woman head of the African Union, and Ngcuka as the first African to lead UN Women.

In 2007 one of the league's most tireless leaders and spokespeople, Mavivi Myakayaka-Manzini, asked the organisation for support. She alleged that her husband, the head of the National Intelligence Agency, Manala Manzini, had been subjecting her to persistent physical abuse. (Later, in divorce proceedings, Manala Manzini would claim that she refused to cook or iron for him and that she talked down to him.) Going public was a shocking move by someone who had been part of the movement for most of her life and was known for her discretion. Yet, her appeal for help reflected the familial nature of relationships in the movement and, given the league's explicit opposition to abuse and violence, was a legitimate approach. Myakayaka-Manzini was the brains behind the Progressive Women's Movement, which she helped to found in 2006 and which was aimed at filling the gap left by the collapse of the Women's National Coalition. It was the leading vehicle for the expansion of the league's influence in civil society. By this stage, however, Myakayaka-Manzini was on the wrong side of the powerful in the league. She opposed the league's support for Jacob Zuma publicly, and argued that the nomination by the league of Zuma as the preferred candidate for ANC president was not in line with the interests of its members. She got no open support from the league during her divorce; it was a private matter, according to Charlotte Lobe, the league spokesperson. That was not entirely surprising to cynical observers; after all, the league had also publicly supported the husband of its executive member and later Minister of International Relations, Maite Nkoane-Mashabane. Norman Mashabane was a diplomat in the Far East with a reputation for womanising; he was found guilty of sexual harassment of a colleague by the Department of Foreign Affairs. Apparently, the leadership of the league could not take a consistent position, even on the most uncontroversial aspects of its platform of action, when the issue was tied to party matters.

The new centre of power in the league was led by Bathabile Dlamini and Angie Motshekga, who were openly allied with Zuma. In November 2007, at a provincial conference of the league in the Northern Cape, representative of branches attacked each other physically, throwing chairs and punches over whether to support Zuma or Mbeki. By the end of that month, in a tightly fought battle, Angie Motshekga's side had won and Zuma was endorsed as president.

9

Feminists versus the league

The Zuma–Mbeki battle was corrosive enough in terms of the collateral damage to the ANCWL. Far more lasting would be the impact of Zuma's leadership on the public debate about the position of women in South African society. The turning point was the trial of Jacob Zuma for rape in 2006, which catapulted issues of gender equality and sexuality into public debate in dramatically new ways.

Early in 2006, Zuma was accused of rape by a woman who occasionally lived in his extended household and was the daughter of Zuma's friend. Khwezi (the pseudonym she used during the trial) alleged that Zuma had entered the room she was sleeping in, got into her bed and had sex with her without her permission and against her wishes. In his defence, Zuma claimed that Khwezi had indicated her sexual availability in a variety of ways and that he did not believe that she was unwilling to have sex with him. In his view, she was bringing the case as part of a political conspiracy against him. In the trial itself, Zuma chose to speak in Zulu and based his defence on the ways in which he interpreted Zulu culture, against Khwezi's invocation of the rights accorded women in the Constitution. The court found that Khwezi was an unreliable witness and found Zuma not guilty.

The trial exposed crucial divisions among supporters of the ANC, and between the ANCWL and women's organisations in civil society. Khwezi's experiences resonated with many organisations that had been dealing for years with rising levels of sexual violence, some of it driven by homophobia, and they were determined to use the case to break the silence surrounding rape and sexual assault. Supporters of Zuma lined up against his detractors outside the court house, with Zuma supporters invoking violent language and abuse in their chants and on their posters (such as 'Burn the bitch'). Perhaps most surprising was the number of women in the ANC who took their place on the side of Zuma rather than Khwezi. Some of these female ANC members held banners that said 'Zuma, rape me'.

Zuma's supporters cast any critique of his behaviour into a theory of political conspiracies. Interestingly, though, they also drew attention to the failings of the new democracy under the presidency of Thabo Mbeki in ways that might lead an observer to think they were from an altogether different political party. They complained about Mbeki's economic policies and impoverishment, about the marginalisation and exclusion of the poor, and the perceived arrogance of the new political and economic elite. Zuma joined his supporters outside the court every day, defiantly singing liberation songs, including 'Bring me my machine gun', a song sung to the action of firing an AK-47 and reinforcing a form of masculinist militant politics contrary to the ethos of the 'women-friendly' pretensions of the ANC government. In any case, as many feminist commentators both inside and outside the ANC pointed out, the reassertion of a form of politics that celebrated phallic symbols and glamorised violence was part of the same syndrome that justified attacks on women.

Feminist activists mobilised by the newly formed One in Nine Campaign supported Khwezi and used the trial as an opportunity to protest against the high levels of violence against women. The feminist banners highlighted the new rights women had acquired in the Constitution. The ANC Women's League issued a statement of 'regret' and 'sadness' at the rape charge, but was not visible outside the court. Indeed, the silence that followed the league's initial statement was most likely a product of tensions between feminists and party loyalists inside the organisation. Memorably, Pumla Dineo Gqola described the outnumbered feminists in the Women's League as 'a handful in a gangrenous sea'.

At no point did Zuma stop his supporters from their brutal verbal and at times physical treatment of Khwezi as she entered the courtroom (at one point an object was thrown her way; at another an effigy of Khwezi was burned outside the court) or from yelling abuse and threats at the feminists across the street. For the duration of the trial, Khwezi was secluded in a safe house under police protection; following the trial she left the country. Zuma, on the other hand, won a massive victory over Thabo Mbeki at the December 2007 ANC conference in Polokwane. His accession to the presidency of the party was supported by the ANC Women's League, and led ultimately to the sacking of Mbeki as President of the country. The ANCWL's reputation as defender of the rights of women, already shaky, had been irretrievably shattered.

Things would only get worse. In August 2009 the Minister of Women, Youth, Children and People with Disabilities, Lulu Xingwana, walked out of an exhibition entitled *Innovative Women*. The exhibition included images by the photographer and lesbian activist Zanele Muholi and the artist Nandipha Mntambo. Muholi's photographs show nude and semi-nude lesbian couples in embrace, and are among her most tender images; in other exhibitions she has portrayed heteronormative violence in images that tend to shock. Nandipha Mntambo's *Rape of Europa* is a deeply symbolic work in which she depicts herself in the twin roles of minotaur and maiden, suggesting the complexities of sexual desire in a patriarchal world.

Xingwana claimed to be offended because the images were pornographic, 'immoral ... and going against nation-building'. Ironically, the exhibition was sponsored by Xingwana's government department and was part of the celebration of Women's Month, a series of activities held every year to honour the contribution of women to South African society. The exhibition was doubtless unsettling to those for whom the narrative of democracy is twinned with the celebration of the presence of women in government. To note the dissonances in democracy – the violence towards those who choose to live outside the given forms of gender, or who articulate intimacies that defy the pristine images of virtuous maternalist politics – is to disrupt the very core of the nation. Xingwana was stung by the criticisms, but her defence did little to encourage debate. She said, 'I was particularly revolted by an image called 'Self-rape' [by Mntambo] ... The notion of self-rape trivializes the scourge of rape in this country.' Just as the Film and Publication Board would do two years later, she drew on the idea of protecting children from pornography to justify her response. 'My reaction was guided by the view that these "artworks" were not suitable for a family audience ... To my mind these were not works of arts [sic] but crude misrepresentations of women (both black and white) masquerading as artworks rather than engaged in questioning or interrogating ... These particular works of art stereotyped black women ... we have laws in this country that protect children against exposure to pornographic material.'

This response by a leading member of the ANC Women's League was a clear statement of the ways in which discourses of equality can conceal the conservative foundations of nationalism and social cohesion. The task of women, as described by Xingwana, is to protect children from the immorality of nudity and intimacy: and, by extension, to stabilise the heterosexual patriarchal family. In this framing, the performance of gender in the public sphere – more specifically, the performance of the category 'woman' – must stabilise both the hetero body form as well as the ideological meaning of female identity as primarily maternal. Xingwana's inability to grasp the ways in which the works of Muholi and Mntambo disrupt the certainties of fixed identities attached to heteronormative patriarchy reveals the limits of a state-sponsored feminism that is detached from the complexities of power relations in society. Neither the ANC Women's League nor Xingwana demonstrates what the Indian scholar Nivedita Menon describes as 'seeing like a feminist': 'to see like a feminist is not to stabilize, it is to destabilize'.

In 2012, when Brett Murray's painting of the President – *The Spear* – became a national cause célèbre, it was again the Women's League that stood at the forefront of the defence of Zuma, dressed in uniform and selling food at the march on the Goodman Gallery. The league called the painting 'an insult to all patriotic South Africans', and accused Murray of disrespecting all the codes of seniority and authority in a homogenised black culture. As one woman said, 'We're supporting Zuma because he's like our father, and the country's father.' She herself was of an age to be a grandmother.

One could read the ANC Women's League's defence of Zuma both at his rape trial and in the *Spear* carnival as a form of complicity with patriarchy in defence of the nation, or an example of what Anne McClintock calls 'designated agency'. Even though the league played a central role in establishing the normative consensus of the secular, universalist democratic value framework of the 1996 Constitution, it seems willing to trade this away for political survival. That survival is dependent on the hollowed-out idea of representation in the state, and in the proportional representation system used in South Africa the league's leaders are most secure when they have the favour of the party. Standing by Zuma for political expedience has, however, come at the price of building a more robust debate on what it might mean to treat women as full political subjects. Instead, both male and female politicians have reinforced the idea of women as inert mimics of male ambitions or agendas.

Under Zuma's presidency, the legislative tide also turned against women as new bills were introduced that would put the project of universal equality on the back foot. Accommodations between the ruling party and traditional leaders even under a democracy with high

143

levels of representation of women have – surprisingly, given that this is the key subject of the politics of the league – imperilled the rights of black rural women. The maintenance and reinvention of traditional systems of governance through legislation such as the Traditional Courts Bill mean that rural black women continue to contend with systems of governance based on the denial of equality – something their urban sisters do not have to face. Aninka Claassens argues that the Traditional Courts Bill – deeply unpopular, as seven of nine provinces have in fact refused to ratify it, thereby demonstrating an awareness that outstrips that of the league – gives chiefs autocratic power over people living in tribal jurisdictions that is even more widespread than the power they had under the apartheid system. Again, it seemed that the ANCWL did not have sufficient power to shape ANC policies, as the bill went through the party structures apparently without the league's capacity to stop it. It is not the case that the league supported this measure, even though this might be the view of its critics, as Lulu Xingwana has been vociferous in her critique, but that their opposition was inaudible. Their impotence throws into question whether their choice of allies within the party has served the cause of gender equality at all.

In the face of growing criticism from civil society activists about the weakness of their representation of poor women's interests in parliament, and the failure of the national machinery to do anything meaningful to address gender inequalities, the league decided to call for the establishment of a Ministry of Women's Affairs. This idea had been mooted and dismissed in the early 1990s by women's organisations, as it was felt then that a single ministry would be ineffective and would create a policy ghetto in which token programmes would be established for women rather than a wide-ranging and systematic redistribution of public funds. Instead, a multi-pronged set of structures was established, designed to strengthen the presence of women in all the key decision-making areas of the state.

In May 2009, at the behest of the league, the Zuma administration changed the architectural design of the machinery by introducing a Ministry of Women, Youth, Children and People with Disabilities. This gave effect to a resolution adopted at the 2007 Polokwane conference, where the ANC Women's League argued in favour of a new institutional framework. The rationale for the new structure was that it would overcome the financial and human resource constraints that plagued the previous structures in government and would carry sufficient authority to implement programmes. The Joint Monitoring Committee was replaced with two committees, a Portfolio Committee on Women, Youth, Children and People with Disabilities in the National Assembly, and a Select Committee on Women, Youth and the Disabled in the National Council of Provinces.

The first minister, Noluthando Sibiya-Mayende,

failed to set up a functional ministry and the league pushed for the appointment of Lulu Xingwana as the new minister. Yet even under Xingwana the ministry remains underfunded and rudderless, with little to show for the money allocated to the department. The ministry was too new and too weak to make any impact on the deliberations of the National Policy Commission, which was engaged in defining the future economic strategy for the country. The failure of the league to ensure that concerns about the status of women would be addressed in the National Development Plan was in striking contrast to the impact of women's organisations on the formulation of the Reconstruction and Development Programme (RDP) in the early 1990s. In that process, feminists had a clear space and voice, and although the RDP was virtually abandoned once the business of ruling began, it was inconceivable then that there could be any plan without attention to gender equality.

Instead of defining a clear programme for addressing inequalities, the league's strategic response has been to demand more space for itself within the government rather than build its political organisation and voice through association with women's organisations in civil society. This time it proposed the enactment of a law that would guarantee gender equality. The oddly named Women Empowerment and Gender Equality Bill was announced on National Women's Day 2012 and proposes two interventions: 'the purpose of the new Bill is to establish a legislative framework for the empowerment of women and to provide an obligation to adopt and implement gender mainstreaming. The Bill includes detailed provisions regarding these issues such as encouraging the recognition of the economic value of the roles of women in various sectors of life, and the achievement of at least 50% representation and participation of women in decision-making structures in all entities.' Coupling representation and accountability is interesting on the face of it and seems to accord with feminist approaches. But the implication is that the very government introducing the bill is the one that needs external mechanisms to ensure compliance with its own policies – it is a politically schizophrenic bill in that respect, part of the Alice in Wonderland politics that has characterised the league's approach to gender equality in the past few years. In effect, it asks the law to do what it could not achieve through its own political power.

10

Where to?

As a vehicle for gender equality, the ANC Women's League has been far from a trusty ship. At many points in its history, the sentimental attachment of gender equality advocates and feminists in the ANC to the organisation has pushed them into working with or in the league. Time and again, feminists have retreated, defeated, and regrouped in other parts of the ANC and in civil society. It is apparent that the league is not the home of South African feminism, however broadly feminism is defined.

Yet it is still an organisation that cannot be dismissed. For, contrary to the critics, it wields a certain degree of power in the party that is most committed to gender equality on the African continent, flawed as its recent record may be. The league is the main gatekeeper for positions in government and parastatal organisations occupied by women. This is not insignificant in a country where targets and quotas for gender representation permeate all policy domains. It is also symbolically important when it comes to the selection of party leaders. This makes it even more perplexing that the league does not see the inherent contradictions in its support for leaders who stand for values diametrically opposed to its policies.

The league's weaknesses go much further. It has not been able to define a policy agenda that addresses gender inequalities, nor has it systematically pursued the opportunities opened up by its strategic association with party leadership to make significant proposals for the redistribution of resources. Indeed, a harsh assessment might be that it has actively undermined the possibility that the national gender machinery might make any difference to the priorities of government.

Even with the limited success that can be attributed to the league, such as the increased numerical representation of women in government and parliament, the current leadership seems set to squander its advantage. In the run-up to the 2014 election it has announced that it will not be putting forward a woman candidate for president. It argues, probably correctly, that the country is not yet ready for a female candidate. It does not ask, though, why sexist attitudes (let alone a much deeper system of patriarchy) persist so far into democracy. It does not ask what it has done, as the self-appointed vanguard of the women's movement, to change those attitudes and defend the constitutional value of equality in the public sphere. Indeed, it does not reflect on its own complicities in advancing a violent, homophobic and sexist culture in the country.

Perhaps fortunately, the struggle for gender equality is not totally subsumed in the organisational form of the Women's League. Pro-equality organisations are regrouping across society – from the One in Nine campaign, and Sonke Gender Justice, to the Forum for the Empowerment of Women, to name just three – and there is a revitalised sense that the process of building democracy needs to be accelerated. In that process, the league has been the loser, as grassroots movements organise not only independently but at times against the league, even within the ANC.

A longer view of the ANC Women's League shows that it was ever thus.

Bibliographic note

There is a growing body of literature on women's organisations and gender politics in South Africa. This is not an exhaustive bibliography but a guide to the key texts that have shaped this book.

The three authoritative analyses of the early part of the twentieth century are:

Iris Berger, *Threads of Solidarity: Women in South African Industry, 1900–1980*, Bloomington: Indiana University Press, 1992

Cherryl Walker, *Women and Resistance in South Africa*, London: Onyx Press, 1982 (republished in South Africa by David Philip in 1991)

Julia C. Wells, '*We Now Demand!*' *The History of Women's Resistance to Pass Laws in South Africa*, Johannesburg: University of the Witwatersrand Press, 1993

See also:

Natasha Erlank, 'Masculinity and Nationalism in South African Nationalist Discourse, 1912–1950', *Feminist Studies* 29, 3 (2003), 653–72

Nomboniso Gasa (ed.), *Women in South African History: Basus' iimbokodo, Bawel' imilambo / They remove boulders and cross rivers*, Cape Town: HSRC Press, 2007

Women's role in Umkhonto we Sizwe is covered in:

Jacklyn Cock, *Colonels and Cadres: War and Gender in South Africa*, Cape Town: Oxford University Press, 1991

For the latter half of the twentieth century I have drawn on my own archival research and interviews conducted for my book *Contesting Authority: Women's Organizations and Democracy in South Africa*, Madison: University of Wisconsin Press. Chapters 4–7 above are excerpted from this book and full references to the quotations may be found there.

For discussions of internal women's organisations, see in addition:

Gertrude Fester, 'Women's Organisations in the Western Cape: Vehicles for Gender Struggle or Instruments of Subordination?', *Agenda* 34 (1997), 45–61

Amanda Kemp, Nozizwe Madlala, Asha Moodley and Elaine Salo, 'The Dawn of a New Day: Redefining South African Feminisms', in Amrita Basu (ed.), *The Challenge* of Local Feminisms: Women's Movements in Comparative Perspective, Boulder: Westview Press, 1995

Susie Nkomo, 'Organising Women in SANSCO: Reflections on the Experience of Women in Organisation', Agenda 10 (1991), 10–15

Leila Patel, 'South African Women's Struggles in the 1980s', Agenda 2 (1988), 28–35

Gay Seidman, '"No Freedom Without the Women": Mobilization and Gender in South Africa, 1970–1992', Signs: Journal of Women in Culture and Society 18, 2 (1993), 210–39

On the transitional period, see:

Catherine Albertyn, 'Women and the Transition to Democracy in South Africa', in Felicity Kaganas and Christina Murray (eds.), Gender and the New South African Legal Order, Cape Town: David Philip, 1995

Susan Bazilli (ed.), Putting Women on the Agenda, Johannesburg: Ravan Press, 1991

Pat Horn, 'Post-apartheid South Africa: What about Women's Emancipation?', Transformation 15 (1991), 26–39

Sheila Meintjes, 'The Women's Struggle for Equality during South Africa's Transition to Democracy', Transformation 30 (1996), 47–64

On the post-apartheid period, see:

Hannah Britton, Women in the South African

Parliament: From Resistance to Governance, Urbana-Champaign: University of Illinois Press, 2005

Hannah Britton, Jennifer Fish and Sheila Meintjes (eds.), *Women's Activism in South Africa: Working across Divides*, Scottsville: University of KwaZulu-Natal Press, 2009

Amanda Gouws (ed.), *(Un)Thinking Citizenship: Feminist Debates in Contemporary South Africa*, Cape Town: Juta, 2005

Sheila Meintjes, 'Gender Equality by Design: The Case of South Africa's Commission on Gender Equality', *Politikon* 32, 3 (2005)

Gay Seidman, 'Institutional Dilemmas: Representation versus Mobilization in South Africa's Gender Commission', *Feminist Studies* 29, 3 (2003), 541–63

Index

9 780821 421567